Transmutation
Taking Your Business From Lead to Gold

By

The Alchemist Professors

Sydney Scott, D.Ed., M.B.A., CPCC
Larry Earnhart, Ph.D., M.B.A.
Shawn Ireland, M.S., M.A. Ed.D.

Edited By Alexandra Pett, Ph.D.

GW00697102

This work incorporates material licensed from:

Leader Publishing Worldwide
19 Axford Bay
Port Moody, BC V3H 3R4
Tel: 1 888 294 9151
Fax: 1 877 575 9151
Website: www.noresults-nofee.com

SYDNEY SCOTT, LARRY EARNHART & SHAWN IRELAND

Published by:
Corporate Alchemy, Inc.
3657 Edgemont Ave.
North Vancouver, BC V7R 2P6
Website: www.thealchemistprofessors.com

While every attempt has been made to verify information provided in this book, neither the author nor the publisher assumes any responsibility for any errors, omissions or inaccuracies.

Any slights of people or organizations are unintentional. If advice concerning legal or related matters is needed, the services of a qualified professional should be sought. This book is not intended as a source of legal or accounting advice. You should be aware of any laws which govern business transactions or other business practices in your state or province.

The examples are not intended to represent or guarantee that everyone will achieve the same results. Each individual's success will be determined by his or her desire, dedication, effort, and motivation. There are no guarantees you will duplicate the results stated here, you recognize that any business endeavor has inherent risk for loss of capital.

Any reference to any persons or business, whether living or deceased, existing or defunct, is purely coincidental.

First Printing October, 2013

ISBN 978-0-9921095-0-9

PRINTED IN CANADA

Acknowledgements

We wish to acknowledge our students, past, present, and future and all those who have learned from us just as we have learned from them. We also want to thank our loved ones, Leslie, Ian and Sue who have stood by us and believed in us while we created this book. With special thanks to Alex Pett whose editing skills par excellence made this book what it is.

To Your Success,

Sydney Scott, Larry Earnhart and Shawn Ireland

Contents

List Of Tables

Alchemy: The Art of Turning Lead Into Gold in Business and in Life

When we first started working together as the Alchemist Professors little did we realize just how much influence we could have on the lives of the people we would be working with. It is very humbling to know that the knowledge and understanding we have gleaned during our lives can be passed on to others who in turn have their lives changed for the better.

The principles outlined in this book represent some of the knowledge base that we want to pass on not just to our clients but to also anybody who can benefit from changing their mindset and behavior.

Perhaps you became an entrepreneur because you felt you had a superior product or service but then realized that running a business keeps taking you further and further away from the ideals you started with. If so, you will need to start with reflection, writing, communicating with yourself and others, and creating new visions for both your life and your business.

By taking the steps outlined in this book, you will reach a wider audience with less effort and less cost realizing greater profits and more time to do what you want to do. This book is organized so that you can begin to read where you want, snack a bit, and then reread as necessary. Feel free to read the chapters in whatever order fits your needs.

We welcome you to this plan you rebrand yourself and transform your business. We hope that the concept of transmutation will work for you as it has for us.

The best time to start is NOW, not tomorrow, not next week or next year.

Yours in success,

Syd, Larry & Shawn

PS. If you would like to arrange a meeting to get a profitable perspective on your business, please send an email to thealchemistprofessors@gmail.com and we will gladly discuss what we can do to help you out.

For a Free Test Drive of all our best tips, tricks and marketing resources visit www.AlchemistBusinessAcademy.com and our corporate website www.TheAlchemistProfessors.com.

1

"Mindset" And The Role
Of The Alchemist

While perusing the self-help sections of several book stores recently we thought about the fact that the hallmark of this literary genre is to offer simplicity, relevance and validity of ideas coupled with recipes for success. Tools, techniques and insights are proffered providing roadmaps for you to become the "alchemist" of your own success.

Upon reflection, we realised that there is no evidence of lasting behavioural and attitudinal change for the readers of these books. At most only 20% of the population are self-changers. This is due, in part, to the behaviour-specific and information-based approaches offering quick-fix formulas to complex problems. Missed in many of these formulas is an appreciation of the complex and contradictory nature of experience, environment and psychology to generate and sustain new ideas and behaviours over time.

Research into sustainable behavioural change identifies the power of self-limiting assumptions to shape our understanding of events and our response to them. Assumptions, often uncritically assimilated and taken-for-granted, are shaped by life experience, our mental health and the impact of our family and culture. Assumptions are rooted in our ***mindset*** or cognitive experience -- how we speak to ourselves and how we "frame" our experience.

Your mindset directly influences the sustainability of any behavioural change. Mindset may be spontaneous (by default) or re-flective (by learning) in response to events or situations. A default mindset offers the comfort of repetition and consistency whilst a learning mindset challenges the assumptions inherent in our views and assessments. It challenges and possibly reframes assumptions to focus on potential and opportunity. For a student is receiving a C+ on a paper an unhelpful criticism (the default mindset) or is it an op-portunity to develop and grow further (the learning mindset)?

The alchemy of the learning mindset is curiosity. Being curi-ous about your mindset, pondering alternative points of view, chal-lenging taken-for granted assumptions informing those views and considering alternative perspectives delivers consistent, long-term behavioural change.

In a recent coaching session with the Alchemist Professors, one of our clients struggled to see the relevance of a new piece of software to her work as a Chartered Accountant. She insisted the software was more complex and cumbersome than was necessary to deliver the documents it generated. She offered complete, coherent, logical and monetary arguments for not using the software but was told by her direct manager the software was to be used nonetheless.

My client learned the basic software protocols but did not adopt the software in its entirety. A year after adoption of the software, my client was offered an opportunity to make recommendations to enhance its efficiency and application. She declined "out of principle!" and could not understand why her manager reacted negatively to her decision.

We discussed how her assumptions shaped her mindset and the response to the request of her supervisor for recommendations. What emerged was an appreciation of self-limiting assumptions to shape her interest in and response to a request -- how the default mindset limits curiosity and interest in exploring the possible.

Recent advances in neuro-science note sustainable learning reflects a mix of curiosity, risk, action and reflection. Consider the following scenario:

> You are driving on your usual route to work. The way is well worn and comfortable, requiring little, if any concentration. You may even get to your office not even realizing how you got there. One day, there is a horrible accident ahead and the path is blocked. However, you must still get to your destination. You consider your options. You can sit and wait it out not knowing when you will move and perhaps be late to work. You can turn around and go home, retreating and deferring as a response. You may consider taking a new path as a response. Both are passive and reflect a default mindset. In order to get to work on time you may create a new pathway. This takes curiosity, risk, action and reflection to plan, execute and finish. Once completed you now have a new experience and new behaviours to consider. But to sustain this new pathway, to memorize and and use it, it is necessary to create opportunities to apply it again and again.

New trails are new neuro-pathways. To sustain new trails requires having the tools and opportunity to apply them again and again. A learning mindset emerges from this opportunity. Mistakes are common, overconfidence typical, incomplete actions unavoidable and **learning inevitable**. The alchemist seeks out new environments to be curious, to take risk, plan actions and then reflect on the outcomes of making these new trails.

You may have experienced being asked by a manager or as a manager requesting a person attend a professional development session. What was your initial reaction or the reaction of the other person to the request? Was it interest or disinterest? Was it viewed as an opportunity or a required activity?

When leading professional development sessions, we witness from the beginning of a session the default mindset of interest or disinterest and its impact on what is taken away from the session. One of our goals as facilitators and educators is to foster an environment where curiosity becomes a natural part of the participant's experience. Offering opportunities for participants to identify self-limiting assumptions that inhibit reflecting on different ideas or points of view is at the core of our work at the Alchemist Professors. Whilst this appears to be a self-evident part of education, in practice managing mindsets is the core challenge we have to address in our practice.

It is difficult to argue with the core ideas of the *learning mindset* or your role as your own alchemist. To argue against these ideas implies rigidity or mental laziness. Yet the premise of the two mindsets offers inconsistencies. These include the default mindset of diminishing perseverance and resilience, inaccuracy of thought and limiting learning and growth. Overlooked in this formulation is our assessment of the relative value associated with the consistency and comfort of the default mindset.

The role interdependency plays in relationships and social contracts, the possibility of psychological comfort and security offered by the default mindset and the benefit of retaining assumptions in the face of minimal opportunities to act, can demonstrate awareness, mindfulness and, even growth. Furthermore, learning can be an outcome of both mindsets in response to the relative value a person places on the mindset in a given situation.

This is not to undermine the value of being aware of mindsets or the role being an alchemist offers us. At the core, the value of challenge the assumptions that limit our avenues for action, the ability to reframe the views derived from the assumptions and the impact of self awareness, are powerful activities to shape behaviours and understanding of what it means to be the alchemist of your success.

2

Use Goal Setting Effectively

We've all heard about the power of setting goals. Everyone has surely seen statistics that connect goal setting to success in both your business life, and your personal life. I'm sure if I asked you today what your goals are, you could rattle off a few wants and hopes without thinking too long.

However, what most people do not realize is that the power of goal setting lies in *writing goals down*. Committing goals to paper and reviewing them regularly gives you a 95% higher chance of achieving your desired outcomes. Studies have shown that only three to five percent of people in the world have written goals – the same three to five percent who have achieve success in business and earn considerable wealth.

This chapter focuses on the power of goal setting as part of your business success. We'll teach you to set **SMART** goals that are rooted in your own personal value system, and supporting techniques to achieve your goals faster.

What are Goals?

Goals are clear targets that are attached to a specific time frame and action plan; they focus your efforts, and drive your motivation in a clear direction. Goals are different from dreams in that they outline a plan of action, while dreams are a conceptual vision of your wish or desired outcome.

Goals require work; work on yourself, work for your business, and work for others. You cannot achieve a goal – no matter how badly you want it – without being prepared to make a considerable effort. If you are ready to invest your time and energy, goals will help you:

- Realize a dream or wish for your personal or business life
- Make a change in your life – add a positive, or remove a negative
- Improve your skills and performance ability
- Start or change a habit – positive or negative

Why Set Goals?

As we've already reviewed, setting goals and committing them to paper is the most effective way to cultivate success. The most important reason to set a goal is **to attach a clear action plan to a desired outcome.**

Goals help focus our time and energy on one (or several) key outcomes at a time. Many business owners have hundreds of ideas whirring around in their heads at any one time, on top of daily responsibilities. By writing down and focusing on a few ideas at a time, you can prioritize and concentrate your efforts, avoid being stretched too thin, and produce greater results.

Since goals attach action to outcomes, goals can help to break down big dreams into manageable (and achievable) sections. Creating a multi-goal strategy will put a road map in place to help you get to your desired outcome. If your goal is to start a pizza business and make six figures a year, there are a number of smaller steps to achieve before you achieve your end result.

Success doesn't happen by itself. It is the result of consistent and committed action by an individual who is driven to achieve something. Success means something different for everyone, so creating goals is a personal endeavor. Goals can be large and small, personal and public, financial and spiritual. It is not the size of the goal that matters; what matters is that you write the goal down and commit to making the effort required to achieve it.

Research has found that establishing goals with support such as a hiring a business coach are far more effective than any other approach to goal setting. Less than 20% of the population is self-changing: each goal changed requires a change in direction along with an expenditure of energy. The most reliable process for goal achievement is the accountability and non-judgmental support that comes from coaching. Add to that the ability to educate on the whys and hows and the goals become obtainable.

The Alchemist Professors, with their various programs and means of supporting you and your staff in creating change and attaining goals provide business owners the help they need.

What happens when I achieve a goal?

You should congratulate yourself and your team, of course! By rewarding yourself and your team after every achievement, you not only train your mind to associate hard work with reward, but develop loyalty among your employees.

You should also ask yourself if your achievement can be taken to the next level, or if your goal can be stretched by building on the effort you have already made. Consistently setting new and higher targets will lay the framework for constant improvement and personal and professional growth.

Power of Positive Thinking

When was the last time you tuned into your internal stream of consciousness? What does the stream of thoughts that run through your mind sound like? Are they positive? Negative? Are they logical? Reasonable?

Positive thinking and healthy self-talk are the most important business tools you can ever cultivate; by programming a positive stream of subconscious thoughts into your mind, you can control your reality, and ultimately your goals. Think about someone you know who is constantly negative; someone who complains and whines and makes excuses for their unhappiness. How successful are they? How do their fears and doubts become reality in their world?

You are what you continuously believe about yourself and your environment. If you focus your mind on something in your mental world, it will nearly always manifest as reality in your physical world.

Positive thinking is a key part of setting goals. You won't achieve your goal until you believe that you can. You will achieve your goals faster when you believe in yourself, and the people around you who are helping to make your goal a reality. The Alchemist Professors website, www.AlchemistProfessors.com, is for clients who can track the habit of positive thinking. This may be the greatest change you or any of your staff can make in their lives and the success of your company. It is a challenging habit to break on one's own as most of us are not conscious that our thoughts are thoughts we choose and we do for the most part have control of them once but only once we can step aside and see them for what they are- waves of energy that dictate the effectiveness of our actions.

Successful people are rooted in a strong belief system – belief in themselves, belief in the work they are doing, and belief in the people around them. They are motivated to improve and learn, but also confident in their existing skills and knowledge. Their positive attitude and energy is clearly felt in everything they do.

Ever notice how complainers usually surround themselves with other complainers? The same is true of positive thinkers. If you cultivate an upbeat and positive attitude, you will be surrounded by people who share your values and outlook on life.

Too often, people and our society subscribe to a continuous stream of negative chatter. The more you hear it, the more you'll believe it.

How many times have you heard:

- That's impossible
- Don't even bother
- It's already been done
- We tried that, and it didn't work
- You're too young
- You're too old
- You'll never get there
- You'll never get that done
- You can't do that

Positive thinking and positive influences will provide the support you need to achieve your goals. Choose your friends and close colleagues wisely, and surround yourself with positive thinkers.

Creating SMART Goals

SMART goals are just that: smart. Whether you are setting goals for your personal life, your business, or with your employees, goals that have been developed with the SMART principle have a higher probability of being achieved.

The SMART Principle

Specific

Specific goals are clearer and easier to achieve than nonspecific goals. When writing down your goal, ask yourself the five "W" questions to narrow in on what exactly you are aiming for. Who? Where? What? When? Why? For example, instead of a nonspecific goal like, "get in shape for the summer," a specific goal would be, "go to the gym three times a week and eat twice as many vegetables."

Measurable

If you can't measure your goal, how will you know when you've achieved it? Measurable goals help you clearly see where you are, and where you want to be. You can see change happen as it happens.

Measurable goals can also be broken down and managed in smaller pieces. They make it easier to create an action plan or identify the steps required to achieve your goal. You can track your progress, revise your plan, and celebrate each small achievement. For example, instead of aiming to increase revenue next year, you would set out to increase revenue by 30% in the next 12 months, and celebrate each 10% along the way.

Achievable

Goals that are achievable have a higher chance of being realized. While it is important to think big, and dream big, too often people set goals that are simply beyond their capabilities and wind up disappointed. Goals can stretch you, but they should always be feasible to maintain your motivation and commitment.

For example, setting a goal to complete your first triathlon but you've never run a mile in your life would be an insurmountable task taken by itself; one that is beyond your current capabilities. If you decide instead to train to run a five kilometer race in three months, a ten kilometer race in six and a half marathon in 12 months then set you would be setting achievable goals that lead you to your ultimate target.

Relevant

Relevant – or realistic – goals are goals that have a logical place in your life or your overall business strategy. The goal's action plan can be reasonably integrated into your life, with a realistic amount of effort.

For example, if your goal is to train to climb to base camp at Mount Everest within one year and you're about to launch a start-up business, you may need to question the relevance of your goal in the context of your current commitments.

Timely

It is essential for every goal to be attached to a time-frame – otherwise it is merely a dream. Check in to make sure that your time-frame is realistic - not too short, or too long. This will keep you motivated and committed to your action plan, and allow you track your progress. Now make yourself and your team members personally accountable to take small steps daily towards these goals.

Autosuggestion + Visualization

Autosuggestion and visualization are two techniques that can assist you in achieving your goals. Some of the most well-known and successful people in the world use these techniques, and it is not coincidence that they are masters in their own fields of business and sport. A few of these people include:

- Michael Phelps (Olympic Swimmer)
- Andre Agassi (Tennis)
- Oprah Winfrey (Entertainment)
- Tiger Woods (Golf)
- Bill Gates (Microsoft)
- Additionally – See book reviews on the Corporate Alchemy web site www.thealchemistprofessors.com
  - Hendricks, The Big Leap (2009)

    o   Seligman, Authentic Happiness: Using the New Positive Psychology to Realize your Potential for Lasting Fulfillment (2012)

Of course, each of these people has a high degree of talent, ambition, intelligence and drive. However, he or she has each used Autosuggestion and Visualization to reach the acme of their respective field.

Autosuggestion

Autosuggestion is your internal dialogue; the constant stream of thoughts and comments that flows through your mind, and impacts what you think about yourself and how you perceive situations.

Since you were a small child, this self-talk has been influenced by your experiences and has programmed your mind to think and react in certain ways. The good news is that you can reprogram your mind and customize your self-talk any way you like. That is the power of Autosuggestion.

To begin practicing Autosuggestion, make sure you are relaxed and open to trying the technique; an ideal time is just before bed, or when you have some time to sit quietly. Then, repeat positive affirmations to yourself about the ideal outcome. Top sports and business people will often practice just before a big game or meeting.

Some examples of positive self-talk or autosuggestion include:

- I will lead my team to a victory tonight!
- I will be relaxed open to meeting new people at the party tonight!
- I will deliver a clear and impacting speech!
- I will stop worrying and tackle this problem tomorrow!
- I will stand up for my own ideas in the meeting!
- I will remember everything I have studied for the test tomorrow!

Visualization

Visualization is a practice complementary to Autosuggestion. While you can repeat affirmations to yourself over and over, combining this practice with visualization is twice as powerful.

Visualization is exactly what it sounds like: repeatedly visualizing how something is going to happen in your mind's eye. Nearly everyone in sports practices this technique. It has been proven to enhance performance better than practice alone.

This technique can easily be applied to business. For example, visualize yourself acting confident and forthright prior to any presentation or meeting where you must speak, present or "perform." You could also visualize yourself being incredibly productive and effective in your office.

Elements to think about during visualization:

- What does the room look like?
- What do the people in the room look like?
- What is their mood? How do they receive me?
- What image do I project?
- How do I look?
- How do I behave? What is my attitude?
- What is the outcome?

Change Is Not Easy

You have to be mentally prepared for change. You may realize that you cannot keep doing the same thing over & over again expecting different results as Albert Einstein once famously said. However, it takes effort over time to realize the fruits of changing your habits. For example, you may have a particular management style that you feel works well but are finding out that your best people leave your business and your customers are unhappy. How do you go about changing your personality traits?

In order to change habits you need to be motivated and persevere. You will have to look for those things that trigger a certain behaviour pattern and overcome them. You will need to repeat your desired behaviour over and over to effect change. And you will need to be mindful of you behaviours. Keep consciously aware of yourself during those times you are performing that task until the change becomes unconscious.

3

Define Your Target Market

Many business owners cannot answer the question: *What is your target market?* They have often made the fatal assumption that *everyone* will want to purchase their product or service with the right marketing strategy.

What is a Target Market?

A target market is simply the group of customers or clients who will likely purchase a specific product or service. This group of people all has something in common, often age, gender, hobbies, or location. Your target market, then, are the people who will buy your offering. This includes both existing and potential customers, all of whom are motivated to do one of three things:

- Fulfill a need
- Solve a problem
- Satisfy a desire

To build, maintain, and grow your business, you need to know who your customers are, what they do, what they like, and why they would buy your product or service. Getting this wrong – or not taking the time to get it right – will cost you time, money, and potentially the success of your business.

The Importance of Knowing Your Target Market

Knowledge and understanding of your target market is the keystone in the arch of your business. Without it, your product or service positioning, pricing, marketing strategy, and eventually, your business could very quickly fall apart.

If you don't intimately know your target market, you run the risk of making mistakes when it comes to establishing pricing, product mix, or service packages. Your marketing strategy will lack direction, and produce mediocre results at best. Even if your marketing message and Unique Selling Proposition (USP) are clear, and your brochure is perfectly designed, it means nothing unless it arrives in the hands (or ears) of the right people.

Determining your target market takes time and careful diligence. While it often starts with a best guess, assumptions cannot be relied on and research is required to confirm original ideas. Your target market is not always your ideal market.

Once you build an understanding of who your target market is, keep up with your market research. Having your finger on the pulse of their motivations and drivers – which naturally change – will help you to anticipate needs or wants and evolve your business.

Types of Markets

Consumer

The Consumer Market includes those consumers who buy products and services for personal use, or for use by family and friends. This is the market category you or I fall into when we're shopping for groceries or clothes, seeing a movie in the theatre, or going out for lunch. Retailers focus on this market category when marketing their goods or services.

Institutional

The Institutional Market serves society and provides products or services for the benefit of society. This includes hospitals, non-profit organizations, government organizations, schools and universities. Members of the Institutional Market purchase products to use in the provision of services to people in their care.

Business to Business (B2B)

The B2B Market is just what it seems to be: businesses that purchase the products and services of other business to run their operations. These purchases can include products that are used to manufacture other products (raw or technical), products that are needed for daily operations (such as office supplies), or services (such as accounting, shredding, and legal).

25

Reseller

This market can also be called the "Intermediary Market" because it consists of businesses that act as channels for goods and services between other markets. Goods are purchased and sold for a profit – without any alterations. Members of this market include wholesalers, retailers, resellers, and distributors.

Determining Your Target Market

Product / Service Investigation

The process for determining your target market starts by examining exactly what your offering is, and what the average customer's motivation for purchasing it is. Start by answering the questions in the Target Market Worksheet on the following page.

Market Investigation

- **In The Field.** Spend some time on the ground researching who your target market might be. If you're thinking about opening a coffee shop, hang out in the neighborhood at different times of the day to get a sense of the people who live, work, and play in the neighborhood. Notice their age, gender, clothing, and any other indications of income and activities.

- **With The Competition.** Who is your direct competitor targeting? Is there a small niche that is being missed? Observing the clientele of your competition can help to build understanding of your target market, regardless of whether it is the same or opposite. For example, if you own a children's clothing boutique and the majority of middle-class mothers

Table 1 Target Market Worksheet

What Basic Need does your product or service meet?	
What Particular Want does your product or service meet?	
What Desire does your product or service fulfill?	
What is the Lifecycle of your product or service?	
What is the Availability of your product or service?	
What is the Cost of the average customer's purchase of your product or service?	
How many times or how often will customers purchase your product or service?	
What upcoming changes do foresee in your industry or region that may affect the sale of your product or service? (positive or negative)	

shop at the local department store, you may wish to focus on higher-income families as your target market.

- **Online.** Many cities and towns – or at least regions – have demographic information available online. Research the ages, incomes, occupations, and other key pieces of information about the people who live in the area you operate your business. From this data, you will gain an understanding of the size of your total potential market.

- **With existing customers.** Talk to your existing customers through focus groups or surveys. This is a great way to gather demographic and behavioral information, as well as genuine feedback about product or service quality and other information that will be useful in a business or marketing strategy.

Who is Your Market?

Based on your Target Market Worksheet results and your product / service and market investigations, you will be able to piece together a basic picture of your target market, and some of their general characteristics. Record some notes in the three Target Market Framework Forms on the next pages. At this point, you may wish to be as specific as possible, or maintain some generalities. You can further segment your market in the next section.

Your Target Market: Putting It Together

Based on the information you gather from your product /
service and market investigations, you should have a clear vision of
your realistic target market. The next pages show examples of how
this information is put together and conclusions are drawn:

Table 2 Consumer Target Market Framework Form

Market Type:	Consumer	
Gender:	☐ Male	☐ Female
Age Range:		
Purchase Motivation:	☐ Meet a Need ☐ Serve a Want ☐ Fulfill a Desire	
Activities:		
Income Range:		
Marital Status:		
Location:	☐ Neighborhood ☐ City ☐ Region ☐ Country	
Other Notes:		

Table 3 Institutional Target Market Framework

Market Type:	Institutional	
Institution Type:	☐ Hospital ☐ School ☐ Charity ☐ Church	☐ Non-profit ☐ University ☐ Government
Purchase Motivation:	☐ Operational Need ☐ Client Want ☐ Client Desire	
Purpose of Institution:		
Institution's Client Base:		
Size:		
Location:	☐ Neighborhood ☐ Region	☐ City ☐ Country
Other Notes:		

Table 4 B2B Target Market Framework

Market Type:	Business to Business (B2B)
Company Size:	
Number of Employees:	
Purchase Motivation:	☐ Operations Need ☐ Strategy ☐ Functionality
Annual Revenue:	
Industry:	
Location(s):	
Purpose of Business:	
People, Culture & Values:	
Other Notes:	

Table 5 Reseller Target Market Framework

Market Type:	Reseller
Industry:	
Client Base:	
Purchase Motivation:	☐ Operations Need ☐ Client Wants ☐ Functionality
Annual Revenue:	
Age:	
Location:	☐ Neighborhood ☐ City ☐ Region ☐ Country
Other Notes:	

Table 6 Target Market Sample 1: Consumer Market

Business: Baby Clothing Boutique	**Business Purpose:** *Meet a need* (provide clothing for infants and children aged 0 to 5 years) *Serve a want* (clothing is brand name only, and has a higher price point than the competition)
Market Type: Consumer	
Gender: Women	
Marital Status: Married	
Market Observations: located on Main Street of Anytown, a street that is seeing many new boutiques open up, proximate to the main shopping mall two blocks from popular mid-range restaurant that is busy at lunch	**Industry Predictions:** large number of new housing developments in the city and surrounding areas two new schools in construction expect to see an influx of new families move to town from Anycity
Competition Observations: baby clothing also available at two local department stores, and one second-hand shop on opposite side of town	**Online Research:** half of Anytown's population is female, and 25% have children under the age of 15 years Anytown's population is expected to increase by 32% within three years The average household income for Anytown is $75,000 annually
TARGET MARKET: The target market can then be described as married mothers with children under five years old, between the ages of 25 and 45, who have recently moved to Anytown from Anycity, and have a household income of at least $100K annually.	

Table 7 Target Market Sample 2: B2B Market

Business: Confidential Paper Shredding	**Target Business Size:** Small to medium
Market Type: B2B (Business to Business)	**Target Business Revenue:** $500K to $1M
Business Purpose: *Meet an operations need* (provide confidential on-site shredding services for business documents)	**Target Business Type:** produce or handle a variety of sensitive paper documentation accountants, lawyers, real estate agents, etc.
Market Observations: there are two main areas of office buildings and industrial warehouses in Anycity three more office towers are being constructed, and will be completed this year	**Industry Predictions:** the professional sector is seeing revenue growth of 24% over last year, which indicates increased client billing and staff recruitment
Competition Observations: one confidential shredding company serves the region, covering Anycity and the surrounding towns provide regular (weekly or biweekly) service, but does not have the capacity to handle large volumes at one time	**Online Research:** Anycity's biggest employment sectors are: manufacturing, tourism, food services, and professional services

TARGET MARKET:

The target market can then be described as small to medium sized businesses in the professional sector with an annual revenue of $500K to $1M who require both regular and infrequent large volume paper shredding services.

Segmenting Your Market

Your market segments are the groups within your target market – broken down by a determinant in one of the following four categories:

- Demographics
- Psychographics
- Geographics
- Behaviors

Segmenting your target market into several more specific groups allows you to further tailor your marketing campaign and more specifically position your product or service. You may wish to divide your ad campaign into four sections, and target four specific markets with messages that will most resonate with the audience.

For example, the baby clothing store may choose to segment its target market by psychographics, or lifestyle. If the larger target market is *married females with children under five, between the ages of 25 and 45, who have a household income of at least $100K annually*, it can be broken down into the following lifestyle segments:

- Fitness-oriented mothers
- Career-oriented mothers
- New mothers

With these three categories, unique marketing messages can be created that speak to the hot-buttons of each segment. The more accurate and specific you can make communications with your target market, the greater impact you will have on your revenues.

Table 8 Market Segmentation Variables

Demographic	Psychographic	Geographic	Behavioristic
Age Income Gender Generation Nationality Ethnicity Marital Status Family Size Occupation Religion Language Education Employment Type Housing Type Housing Ownership Political Affiliation	Personality Lifestyle Values Attitude Motivation Activities Interests	Region Country City Area Neighborhood Density Climate	Brand Loyalty Product Usage Purchase Frequency Profitability Readiness to Buy User Status

Understanding Your Target Market

Once you have determined who your market is, make a point of learning everything you can about it. You need to have a strong understanding of who makes up your target, what they like, where they shop, why they buy, and how they spend their time. Remind yourself that you may *think* you know your market, but until you have verified the information, you'll be driving your marketing strategy blind.

Also be aware that markets change, just like people. Just because you knew your market when you started your business 10 years ago, doesn't mean you know it now. Regular market research is part of any successful business plan, and a great habit to start.

Types of Market Research

Surveys

The simplest way to gather information from your clients or target market is through a survey. You can craft a questionnaire full of questions about your product, service, market demographics, buyer motivations, and so on. Plus, anonymous surveys will produce the most accurate information since names are not attached to the results or specific comments.

Depending on the purpose—whether it is to gather demographic information, product or service feedback, or other data—there are a number of ways to administer a survey.

1. *Telephone*

   Telephone surveys are a more time-consuming option, but have the benefit of live communication with your target market. Generally, it is best to have a third party conduct this type of survey to gather the most honest feedback. This is the method that market researchers use for polling, which can be highly reliable.

2. *Online*

   Online surveys are the easiest to administer yourself. There a many web-based services that quickly and easily allow to you customize your survey, and send it to your email marketing list. These services can also analyze, summarize and interpret the results on your behalf. Keep in mind that the results include only those who are motivated to respond, which may bias your results.

3. *Paper-Based.*

   Paper surveys are seldom used, and can prove to be an inefficient method. Like online surveys, your results are based on the feedback of those who were motivated for one reason or another to respond. However, the time and effort involved in taking the survey, filing it out, and returning it to your place of business may deter people from participating.

   Surveys can be complex to administer and consume more time and resources than you have planned. If you have the budget, consider hiring a professional market research firm to lead or assist with the process. This will also ensure that the methodology is standard practice, and will garner the most accurate results.

Website Analysis

Tracking your website traffic is an excellent way to research your existing and potential customer's interests and behavior. From this information, you can ensure the design, structure and content of your website is catering to the people who use it – and the people you want to use it.

User-friendly website traffic analytics programs can easily show you who is visiting your site, where they are from, and what pages of your site they are viewing. Services like Google Analytics can tell you what page they arrive at, where they click to, how much time they spend on each page, and on which page they leave the site.

This is powerful (and often free!) information to have in your market research, and easy to monitor monthly or weekly, depending on the needs of your business.

Customer Purchase Data (Consumer Behavior)

If you do not have the budget to conduct your own professional market research, you can use existing resources on consumer behavior. While this data may not be specific to your region or city, general consumer research is actual data that can be helpful in confirming assumptions you may have made about your target market.

Your customer loyalty program or Point of Sale system may also be of help in tracking customer purchases and identifying trends in purchase behavior. If you can track who is buying, what they're buying and how often they're buying, you'll have an arsenal of powerful insight into your existing client base.

Focus Groups

Focus groups look at the psychographic and behavioristic aspects of your target market. Groups of six to 12 people are gathered and asked general and specific questions about their purchase motivations and behaviors. These questions could relate to your business in particular, or to the general industry.

Focus group sessions can also be time consuming to organize and facilitate, so consider hiring the services of a professional market research firm. You may also receive more honest information if a third party is asking the questions, and receiving the responses from focus group participants.

For cost savings, consider partnering with an associate in the same industry who is not a direct competitor, and who would benefit from the same market data.

4

Creating a Powerful Offer

I'm not going to beat around the bush on this one:

Your Offer Is The Granite Foundation Of Your Marketing Campaign.

Get it right, and everything else will fall into place. Your headline will grab readers, your copy will sing, your ad layout will hardly matter, and you will have customers running to your door.

Get it wrong, and even the best looking, best-written campaign will sink like the Titanic.

A powerful offer is an irresistible offer. It's an offer that gets your audience frothing at the mouth and clamoring over each other all the way to your door. An offer that makes your readers pick up the phone and open their wallets.

Irresistible offers make your potential customers think, "I'd be crazy not to take him up on that," or "An offer like this doesn't come around very often." They instill a sense of emotion, of desire, and ultimately, urgency.

Make it easy for customers to purchase from you the first time, and spend your time keeping them coming back.

I'll say it again:

Get the offer right, and everything else will fall into place.

The Crux of Your Marketing Campaign

As you work your way through this program, you will find that nearly every chapter discusses the importance of a powerful offer as related to your marketing strategy or promotional campaign.

There's a reason for this. The powerful offer is more often than not the reason a customer will open their wallets. It is how you generate leads, and then convert them into loyal customers. The more dramatic, unbelievable, and valuable the offer is the more dramatic and unbelievable the response will be.

Many companies spend thousands of dollars on impressive marketing campaigns in glossy magazines and big city newspapers. They send massive direct mail campaigns on a regular basis; yet don't receive an impressive or massive response rate.

These companies do not yet understand that simply providing information on their company and the benefits of their product is not enough to get customers to act. There is no reason to pick up the phone or visit the store, *right now*.

Your powerful, irresistible offer can:

- Increase leads
- Drive traffic to your website or business
- Move old product
- Convert leads into customers
- Build your customer database

What Makes a Powerful Offer?

A powerful offer is one that makes the most people respond, and take action. It gets people running to spend money on your product or service. Powerful offers nearly always have an element of *urgency* and of *scarcity*. They give your audience a reason to act immediately, instead of put it off until a later date.

Urgency relates to time. The offer is only available until a certain date, during a certain period of the day, or if you act within a few hours of seeing the ad. The customer needs to act now to take advantage of the offer.

Scarcity related to quantity. There are only a certain number of customers who will be able to take advantage of the offer. There may be a limited number of spaces, a limited number of products, or simply a limited number of people the business will provide the offer to. Again, this requires that customer acts immediately to reap the high value for low cost.

Powerful offers also:

Offer great value. Customers perceive the offer as having great value – more than a single product on its own, or the product at its regular price. It is clear that the offer takes the reader's needs and wants into consideration.

Make Sense To The Reader. They are simple and easy to understand if read quickly. Avoid percentages – use half off or 2 for 1 instead of 50% off. There are no "catches" or requirements; no fine print.

Seem logical. The offer doesn't come out of thin air. There is a logical reason behind it – a holiday, end of season, anniversary celebration, or new product. People can get suspicious of offers that seem "too good to be true" and have no apparent purpose.

Provide A Premium. The offer provides something extra to the customer, like a free gift, or free product or service. They feel they are getting something extra for no extra cost. Premiums are perceived to have more value than discounts.

Remember That When Your Target Market Reads Your Offer, They Will Be Asking The Following Questions:

1. What are you offering me?
2. What's in it for me?
3. What makes me sure I can believe you?
4. How much do I have to pay for it?

The Most Powerful Types of Offers

Decide what kind of offer will most effectively achieve your objectives. Are you trying to generate leads, convert customers, build a database, move old product off the shelves, or increase sales? Consider what type of offer will be of most value to your ideal customers – what offer will make them act quickly.

Free Offer

This type of offer asks customers to act immediately in exchange for something free. This is a good strategy to use to build a customer database or mailing list. Offer a free consultation, free consumer report, or other item of low cost to you but of high perceived value. You can also advertise the value of the item you are offering for free. For example, act now and you'll receive a free consultation, worth $75 dollars. This will dramatically increase your lead generation, and allow you to focus on conversion when the customer comes through the door or picks up the phone.

The Value Added Offer

Add additional services or products that cost you very little, and combine them with other items to increase their attractiveness. This increases the perception of value in the customer's mind, which will justify increasing the price of a product or service without incurring extra hard costs to your business.

Package Offer

Package your products or services together in a logical way to increase the perceived value as a whole. Discount the value of the package by a small margin, and position it as a "start-up kit" or "special package." By packaging goods of mixed values, you will be able to close more high-value sales. For example: including a free desk-jet printer with every computer purchase.

Premium Offer

Offer a bonus product or service with the purchase of another. This strategy will serve your bottom line much better than discounting. This includes 2 for 1 offers, offers that include free gifts, and in-store credit with purchases over a specific dollar amount.

Urgency Offer

Offers that include an element of urgency enjoy a better response rate, as there is a reason for your customers to act immediately. Give the offer a deadline or limit the number of spots available.

Guarantee Offer

Offer to take the risk of making a purchase away from your customers. Guarantee the performance of your product or service, and offer your customers their money back if they are not satisfied. This will help overcome any fear or reservations about your product, and make it more likely for your leads to become customers.

Create Your Powerful Offer

Four steps to creating your offer:

1. Pick A Single Product Or Service.

Focus on only one product or service – or one product or service *type* – at a time. This will keep your offer clear, simple, and easy to understand. This can be an area of your business you wish to grow, or old product that you need to move off the shelves.

2. Decide What You Want Your Customers To Do.

What are you looking to achieve from your offer? If it is to generate more leads, then you'll need your customer to contact you. If it is to quickly sell old product, you'll need your customer to come into the store and buy it. Do you want them to visit your website? Sign up for your newsletter? How long do they have to act? Be clear about your call to action, and state it clearly in your offer.

3. Dream Up The Biggest, Best Offer.

First, think of the biggest, best things you could offer your customers – regardless of cost and ability. Don't limit yourself to a single type of offer, combine several types of offers to increase value. Offer a premium, plus a guarantee, with a package offer. Then take a look at what you've created, and make the necessary changes so it is realistic.

4. Run The Numbers.

Finally, make sure the offer will leave you with some profit – or at least allow you to break even. You don't want to publish an outrageous offer that will generate a tremendous number of leads, but leave you broke. Remember that each customer has an acquisition cost as well as a lifetime value. The amount of their first purchase may allow you to break even, but the amount of their subsequent purchases should make you a lovely profit.

5

Use Scripts to Increase Sales Immediately

What do playbooks, prompts, guides and scripts all have in common?

They are all popular tools that dictate or guide human behavior toward a desired outcome.

Playbooks help coaches tell sports teams specifically how to play the game to overcome an opponent. Prompts help to kick-start writers and other creative professionals when stuck in a rut. Guides provide a series of instructions so that a person or team of people can complete or implement a specific task. Film scripts tell actors how to act for a particular part.

If you're in the business of sales, you also know about sales scripts. Sales scripts are tools that guide salespeople during interactions or conversations with potential customers.

A large number of businesses use scripts, either as a way of maintaining consistency amongst a sales team, training new salespeople, or enhancing their sales skills. They may have a single script, or several, and may change their scripts regularly, or use the same one for years.

What most businesses overlook, however, is that the sales script is a living, breathing, changing member of their sales team. They may be internal documents, but they deserve just as much time and effort as your marketing collateral.

Do You Really Need a Script?

The short answer is yes. You absolutely need a script for any and every customer interaction you and your salespeople may find yourselves in. Sure, countless business owners and salespeople work every day without a script. If you own your own business, chances are you're already a pretty good salesperson. But if you are not using scripts, you're only working at half of your true potential – or half of your potential earnings.

Scripts don't have to be "cheesy" or read verbatim. They act as a map for your sales process, and provide prompts to trigger your memory and keep you on track. How many times have you made a cold call that didn't work out the way you wanted it to? Scripts dramatically improve the effectiveness and efficiency of your sales processes.

A comprehensive set of scripts will also keep a level of consistency amongst your salespeople and the customer service they provide your clients. What we've found at Alchemist Professors is that once scripts are written, memorized, and rehearsed, they become like film scripts; the salesperson can breathe their own life and personality into the conversation, while staying focused on the call's objectives

Why Your Scripts Aren't Working

If you a currently using scripts in your business, are they working? Are they as effective as they could possibly be? How do you know? When was the last time they were reviewed or updated?

Scripts are like any other element of your marketing campaign – they need to be tested and measured for results, and changed based on what is or is not working.

Measure the success of your script based on your conversion rates. Of all the people you speak to and use the script, how many are being converted from leads to sales?

When evaluating your existing scripts, ask yourself the following questions:

How old is this script? What was it written for? Scripts are living, breathing members of your company. They need to be written and rewritten and rewritten again as the needs of your customers change, your product or services change, or as new strategies are implemented.

Does this script address all the customer objections we regularly hear? Every time you hear a customer raise an objection that is not included on the script, add it. The power of your script lies in the ability to anticipate customer concerns, and answer them before they're raised.

Does this script sound the same as the others? Your scripts are part of the package that represents you as a company. There should be a consistent feel or approach throughout your scripts that your customers will recognize and feel confident dealing with.

Is everyone using the script? Who on your team regularly uses these scripts? Just the junior staff? Only the top-performing staff? Make sure everyone is singing from the same song sheet – your customers will appreciate the consistency and will be turned off by the lack thereof.

Types of Scripts

Depending on the product or service you offer and the marketing strategies you have chosen, there are countless types of scripts you could potentially prepare for your business,

When you sit down to create your scripts, it would be wise to start by making a list of all the instances you and your staff members interact with your existing or potential customers. Then, prioritize the list from most to least important, and start writing from the top.

Here are some commonly used scripts, and their purposes:

Sales Presentation Script

Each time you or your sales staff make a presentation, they should be using the same or a slightly modified version of the same script. This script will include sample icebreakers, a presentation on benefits and features of the product or service, and a list of possible objections and responses. These scripts should also help alleviate some of the nervousness or anxiety associated with public speaking.

Closing Script

Closing scripts help you do just that: close the sale. This could include a list of closing prompts or statements to get the transaction started. This type of script also includes a list of possible customer objections, and planned responses.

Incoming Phone Call Script

Everyone who calls your business should be treated the same way; consistent information should be gathered and provided to the customer. The person answering the phone should state the company name, department name, and their own name in the initial greeting. This goes for both the main line, and each individual or department extension.

Cold Call Script

This is one of the most important scripts you can perfect for your business. The cold call script must master the art of quickly getting the attention of the customer, then engaging and persuading them with the benefits of the product or service. The caller needs to establish common ground with the potential customer, and find a way to get them talking through open-ended questions.

Direct Mail Follow-Up Script

Scripts for outgoing calls that are intended to follow up on a direct mail piece are essential for every direct mail campaign. They are designed to call qualified leads that have already received information and an offer, and convert them into customers. These scripts should focus on enticing customers to act, and overcoming any objections that may have prevented them from acting sooner.

Market Research Script

Scripts that are used primarily for the purpose of gathering information should be designed to get the customer talking. A focus on open-ended questions and relationship building statements will help to relax the customer, and encourage honest dialogue.

Difficult Customer Script

Just like every salesperson needs to practice the sales process, you and your staff also need to practice your ability to handle difficult customers. If you operate a retail business this is especially important, as difficult customers often present themselves in front of other customers. These scripts should help you diffuse the situation, calm the customer down, and then handle their objections.

Creating Scripts

Creating powerful scripts is not a complicated exercise, but it will take some time to complete. Focus on the most vital scripts for your business first, and engage the assistance of your sales staff in drafting or reviewing the scripts.

Your Script Binder

Keep master copies of all of your scripts in one organized place. An effective way to do this is to create a binder, and use tabs to separate each type of script.

You will also want to create a separate tab for customer objections, and list every single customer objection you have ever heard in relation to your product or service. Find a way to organize each objection so you can easily find them – group them by category or separate them with tabs.

Then, list your responses next to each objection – there should be several responses to each objection created with different customer types in mind. A master list of customer objections and responses is an invaluable tool for any business owner, salesperson, and script writer. The more responses you can think of, the better.

Remember, the script binder is never "finished." You will need to make sure that it is updated and added to on a regular basis.

Writing Scripts – Step by Step

Step One: Record What You're Doing Now

If you aren't using scripts – or even if you are – start by re-cording yourself in action. Use video or audio recording to tape yourself on the phone, in a sales presentation, or with a customer. Make notes on your body language, word choice, customer reaction and body language, responses to objections, and closing statements.

You may also wish to ask an associate to make notes on your performance and discuss them with you in a constructive fashion.

Step Two: Evaluate What You're Doing Wrong

Take a look at your notes, and ask yourself the following questions:

- How are you engaging the customer?
- Are you building common ground and trust?
- Does what you are saying matter to the customer?
- Is your offer a powerful one?
- What objections are raised?
- How are you dealing with them?
- What objections are you avoiding?
- How natural is your close?
- Are you as effective as you think you can be?

Once you have answered and made notes in response to these questions, make a list of things you need to improve, and how you think you might go about doing so. Do you need to strengthen your closing statements? Do you need to brainstorm more responses to objections? Remember that everyone's script and sales process can be improved.

Step Three: Decide Who the Script is For

So now that you know the elements of your script you need to work on, you can begin drafting your new script, or revising an old one.

The first part of writing a script – or any piece of marketing material – is having a strong understanding of who you are writing it for. Who is your target audience? What does your ideal customer look like? Consider demographic characteristics like age, sex, location, income, occupation and marital status. Be as specific as possible. What are their purchase patterns? What motivates them to spend money?

If you are writing a cold call script, you will need to develop or purchase a list of people who fall into the target market specifics you have established. If you are writing a sales script for in-store customers, then spend some time reviewing what types of customers find their way into your place of business.

You will want to use words that your target audience will not only understand, but relate to and resonate with. Use sensory language that will trigger emotional and feeling responses – *I need this, this will solve that problem, I'll feel better if I have this, etc.*

Step Four: Decide What You Want to Say

There are typically five sections of every script – and there may be more, depending on the type and purpose of script:

1. Engage

- Get their attention or pique their interest
- Establish common ground
- Build trust, be human
- Ask for their time

2. Ask & Qualify

- Control the conversation by asking questions
- Focus on open-ended questions that cannot be answered with a "yes" or "no"
- Get the customer talking
- Ask as many questions as you need to get information on the customer's needs and purchase motivations

3. Get Agreement

- Ask closed-ended questions you are sure they will respond to with "yes"
- Get them to agree on the benefits of the product or service
- Repeat key points back to the customer to gain agreement

4. Overcome Objections

- Anticipate objections based on customer comments, then refute them
- Make informative assumptions about their thought process, identify with their concern, then refute it using your own experiences
- Repeat concerns back to the customer to let them know you have heard them
- Ask about any remaining objections before you close

5. Close

- Assume that you have overcome all objections, and have the sale in hand
- Ask the customer transactional questions, like delivery timing and payment method
- Be as confident and natural as possible

Step Five: Train Your Staff

Once you have written your company's scripts, you will need to ensure your staff understand and are comfortable using them. Consider having a team meeting, and use role play to review each of the scripts. This will encourage your salespeople to practice amongst each other, and strengthen their sales skills. Ask them for feedback on the scripts, and make any necessary changes.

You will also need to decide how comfortable you are having your salespeople personalizing the scripts to suit their own styles.

59

Be clear what elements of the script are "company standards" and essential techniques, but also be flexible with your team.

Step Six: Continually Revise

After you have carefully crafted your script, put it to the test. Practice on your colleagues, friends, and family. Get their feedback, and make changes. Remember that scripts will need to change and evolve as your business changes and evolves, and new products or services are introduced. Keep your script binder on your desk at all times, and continually make changes and improvements to it.

You may also wish to record and evaluate your performance on a regular basis. This is an exercise you could incorporate into regular employee reviews, to use as a constructive tool for staff development.

Script Tips

- Practice anticipating and eliciting real objections – including the ones your customer doesn't want to raise.

- Make the script yours – it should look, feel, and sound like you naturally do, not like you're reading off the page.

- Spend time with the masters. If there is a salesperson you admire ask to observe them in action. Take notes on their performance, and the techniques they use for success.

- If your script is not successful, ask the customer why not? Even if you don't get the sale, you'll get a new objection you can craft responses to and never get stumped by it again.

- Don't fear objections. Just spend time identifying as many as possible, then practice overcoming them.

- Never stop thinking of responses to customer objections. Each objection could potentially have 30 responses, geared toward specific customer types.

- Anecdotes are persuasive writing tools – use them in your scripts. People enjoy hearing stories, especially stories that relate to them and their experiences, frustrations, and troubles. Let the story sell your product or service for you.

- Include body language in your scripts – it's just as important as your words. Try mimicking your subject's posture, arm position, and seating position. This is proven to create ease and build trust.

- If you only have your voice, use it. Pay attention to tone, language choice, speed, and background noise. You only have sound to establish a trusting relationships, so do it carefully.

- Be confident, and focus on a positive stream of self-talk to prepare for the call or presentation. Confidence sells.

- Spend time on your closing scripts, as they are a critical component of your presentation or phone call. This can be a challenging part of the sales process, so practice, practice, practice.

6

How to Double your Referrals

What if I told you that you could put an inexpensive system in place that would effectively allow your business to growth itself?

For most business owners, a large part of their customer base is comprised of referral customers. These people found out about the company's products or services from the recommendation of a friend or colleague who had a positive experience purchasing from that company. If your business benefits from referral customers, you will find that these customers arrive ready to buy from you, and tend to buy more often. They also tend to be highly loyal to your product or service.

Seem like great customers to have, don't they?

Referral customers cost less to acquire. Compared to the leads you generate from advertising, direct mail campaigns, and other marketing initiatives, referral customers come to you already qualified and already trusting in the quality of your offering and the respectability of your staff.

With a little effort, and the creation of a formalized system – or strategy – you can not only continue to enjoy referral business, but easily double the number of referral customers that walk through your door. All of this is possible for a minimal investment of time and resources.

Is Your Business a Referral Business?

Referral based businesses benefit from a stream of qualified customers who arrive at their doorstep ready to spend. These businesses put less focus on advertising to generate new leads, and more focus on serving and communicating with their existing customers.

Generally speaking, a referral program can generate outstanding results for nearly any business. Since most referrals do not require any effort, the addition of a strategy and a program will often double or triple the number of qualified referrals that come through a business door.

There are, however, a few types of businesses that will not benefit from a formalized referral strategy. These are businesses with low price points – like fast food restaurants and drugstores. Their customer base is large already, and their efforts would be best spent on increasing the average sale.

A referral program can:

- **Save You Time**. Referral strategies – once established – don't require much management or time investment.

- **Deliver More Qualified Customers**. Your customer arrives with an assumption of trust, and willing to purchase.

- **Improve Your Reputation.** Your customer's networks likely overlap, and create potential for a single customer to be referred by two people. This encourages the perception that your business is "the place to go."

- **Speed The Sales Process.** You will have existing common ground and a reputation with the referred customer.

- **Increase Your Profit.** You will spend less time and money generating leads, and more time serving customers who have their wallets open.

The Cost of Your Customers

As we discussed in the "Repeat Business" section, you don't "get" customers, you *buy* them. The money you spend on advertising, direct mail, and other promotions ideally results in potential customers walking through your doors.

For example, if you placed an ad for $200, and 20 people make a purchase in response to that ad, you would have paid $10 for each customer.

Referral customers cost you next to nothing. Your existing customer does the work of selling your business to their friend or associate, and you benefit from the sale. Aside from the cost of any referral incentives or coupon production, there is no cost involved at all.

Referral customers cost less and require less time investment than any other customer. That means you can spend that time making them a loyal customer, or a devoted fan.

Groom Your Customers

Referral strategies can allow you to groom your customer base. As we have previously discussed, 80% of your revenue comes from 20% of your customers – these are your ideal customers. These are also the people you have established as your target market, and are the people you cater your marketing and advertising efforts toward.

You also have a group of customers who make up 80% of your headaches. These are the people who complain the most and spend the least.

Use your referral strategy to get more of your *ideal* customers. Spend more time servicing your ideal customers – do everything you can to make them happy – and less time on your headache customers. You can even ask your headache customers to shop elsewhere.

Then, focus your referral efforts on your ideal customers. Ask them to refer business to you, and reward them for doing so.

Try to avoid referrals from your headache customers – chances are you'll just get another headache.

Referral Sources

Take some time to brainstorm all the people who could potentially refer business to you. Think beyond your business, to your extracurricular activities and personal life. There are endless sources of people who are ready and willing to send potential customers your way.

Here are some ideas to get you started:

Past Relationships

No, not romantic relationships! We're talking about anyone you have previously had a business relationship with, but for one reason or another have fallen out of touch. This includes former colleagues, associates, customers and friends.

Including them in your referral strategy can be as simple as reaching out through the phone or email, and updating them on your latest business initiative or career move. Gently ask at the end of the correspondence to refer anyone who may need your product or service. They will appreciate that you have attempted to re-establish the relationship.

Suppliers and Vendors

Your suppliers and vendors can be a great source for referrals, because they presumably deal daily with businesses that are complementary to your own. The opportunities to connect two of their customers in a mutually beneficial relationship are endless. These businesses should be happy to help out - especially if you have been a regular and loyal customer.

Customers

Customers are an obvious source of referrals because they are the people who are dealing with you directly on a regular basis. Often, all you have to do is ask and they will happily provide you with contact information of other interested buyers, or contact those buyers themselves.

Your customers also have a high level of product knowledge when it comes to your business, and are in a great position to really sell the strength of your company. Remember from the Testimonials section, the words of your customers are at least 10 times more powerful than any clever headline or marketing piece you could create.

Employees and Associates

Give your employees and associates a reason to have their friends and families shop at your business with a simple incentive program. These people have the most product knowledge, and are in the best position to sell you to a potential customer.

68

This is also a way to tap into an endless network of people. Who do your employees and associates know? Who do their friends and friends of friends know? A referral chain that connects to your employees can be a highly powerful one.

Competitors

This doesn't seem so obvious, but it can work. Your direct competitors are clearly not the ideal source for referrals. However, indirect competitors can refer their clients or potential clients to you if they cannot meet those clients' needs themselves.

For example, if you sell high end lighting fixtures, the low-budget lighting store down the street may be able to refer clients to you, and vice versa. You may wish to offer a finder's fee or incentive to establish this arrangement.

Your Network

Don't be shy about asking your friends and family members for referrals. Too many people do not provide enough information to their inner circle about what they do or what their business does. This doesn't make sense, since these are the people who should be the most interested!

Take time to explain clearly what your business is all about, and what your unique selling point is. Then just ask them if they know anyone who may benefit from what you are offering. You could even provide your friends and family with an incentive – a gift, a meal, or a portion of the sale.

Associations & Special Interest Groups

This is another place you likely have a network of people who have limited knowledge about what you do or what your business does. The advantage here is that you have a group of people with similar belief s and values in the same room. Use it!

The Media

Unless a member of the media is a regular customer of yours, or you are in business to serve the media, this may not seem like an obvious choice either.

The opportunity here is to establish a relationship with an editor or journalist, and position yourself as an expert in your field or industry. Then, next time they are writing a related story, they can ask to quote you and your opinion. When their audience reads the story, they will perceive your business as the industry leader.

Referral Strategies

A referral strategy is any system you can put in place to generate new leads through existing customers. The ideal way to do this is to create a system that runs itself! Here are some ideas for simple strategies you can begin to implement into your business immediately.

Just Ask

This may seem simple and obvious, but it's true. Be open with your customers and associates, and simply ask them if they can refer any of their friends or associates to you. Make it part of doing business with you, and your customers will grow to expect the question. Or, let them know in advance that you'll be asking at a later date.

Remember that this can include potential customers – even if they don't buy from you. The reason they chose not to purchase may have nothing to do with your business; any person who has begun to or actually done business with you can refer to you another person.

A useful script for asking anybody for a referral is: *"Who else do you know, a friend, family member or coworker, who could use my services? If you give me their name and phone number or email address I will tell them you recommended me to them."* It is better to ask for names instead of asking them to pass on your card or to have them call you as it puts the initiative in your hands.

Many people are reluctant to pass on their close circle of friends and family until you build enough trust with them but all sales comes down to numbers. Ask enough people and you will get results."

Offer Incentives

When you speak to your customers, when you ask them for something, you typically try to answer the question "what's in it for me?" before they ask it.

The same is true when you ask your customers for a referral. Incentive-based referral strategies work wonders, and can easily be implemented as part of a customer loyalty program, or as part of your existing customer relations systems.

Consider offering customers who successfully refer clients to you discounts on products, free products or services, or gifts. Offer incentives relative to the number of referrals, or the success rate of each referral.

This can have a spin off effect, as your referral customers may become motivated to continue the referral chain. They too will be interested in the incentives you have provided, and tell their friends about your business.

Be Proactive

The only way your referral program will work is if you put some effort into it, and maintain some level of ongoing effort.

Here are some ideas:

- Put a referral card or coupon in every shopping bag that leaves your store
- Promote gift certificates during peak seasons
- Offer free information seminars to existing customers, and ask them to bring a friend
- Host a closed-door sale for your top 20 customers and their friends

Provide Great Customer Service

An easy way to encourage referral business is to treat every potential customer with exemplary customer service. Since the art of customer service is lost is many communities, people are often impressed by simple added touches and conveniences. That alone will encourage them to refer your business to their network.

Stay In Touch

Make sure you are staying in touch with all of your potential and converted customers. Through newsletters, direct mail, or the Internet, keep your business name at the top of the minds, ahead of the competition.

Even if they have already purchased from you, and may not need to purchase for some time, a newsletter or email can be a simple reminder that your business is out there. If someone in their network is looking for the product or service, it will be more likely that your customer will refer your business over the competition.

7

How to Create Repeat Business and Have Clients that Pay, Stay and Refer

When it comes to marketing and generating more income, most business owners are focused outward.

They've carefully established and segmented their target market, and created specific offers and messages for each market segment. They spend thousands of dollars in advertising and direct mail campaigns in hot pursuit of more leads, more customers, and more foot traffic.

While this is an effective way to build a business, it is costly and time consuming. It requires constant and consistent effort, and while this approach does generate results, those results quickly disappear when the effort stops or becomes less intense.

Successful businesses that see sustained growth have a double-edged marketing strategy. They focus their efforts *outward* – onto new potential customers and marketing – as well as *inward* – onto existing customers and referral business.

These successful businesses have leveraged their existing efforts to generate more revenue. Simply put, their customers buy from them over and over again.

For most businesses, this is the easiest way to increase their revenues. Simple customer loyalty strategies and outstanding customer service are often all you need to dramatically increase your sales – from the customers you already have.

The Cost of Your Customers

Do you know how much it costs your business to buy new customers? Each new customer that walks through your door – with the exception of referrals – has cost you money to acquire. You have spent money on advertising and promotions to generate leads and turn those leads into customers.

For example, if you have placed an ad in your local newspaper for $1,000, and the ad brings in 10 customers, you have paid $100 to acquire each customer. You would need to ensure each of those customers spent at least $200 to cover your margin and break even.

Alternately, if you spent two hours of your time and $10 per month on an email marketing program to send a newsletter to your existing database of customers, and you bring in 10 customers as a result – each customer has cost you $1.

Generating more repeat business means focusing on the marketing strategies that aim to keep your existing customers instead of purchase new ones – effectively reducing the cost of attracting new customers to your business.

These strategies are simple to implement, and don't require much time investment. Just a solid understanding of how to make customers want to come back and spend more of their money

Keeping Your Customers

Marketing strategies that focus on keeping your current customer base are easy and enjoyable to implement. They allow you to build real relationships with the people you do business with, instead of dealing with a revolving door of people on the other end of your sales process.

Repeat customers create a community of people around your business that presumably share the same needs, desires and frustrations. The information you gain from these customers (market research) can help you strengthen your understanding of your target audience, and more accurately segment it.

Remember – 80% of your revenue comes from 20% of your customers. Always focus on these customers. They are ideal customers that you want to recruit, and hold on to.

Customer Service: Make Them Love Buying From You

Every business – even those with excellent service standards can improve the service they provide their customers. Customer service seems to be a dying concept in most businesses; more focus seems to be placed on the speed of the transaction. These days you can even go to the grocery store now and not speak to a single sales associate thanks to self-serve checkouts.

To improve your company's customer service standards, take a survey of your customers and your employees to brainstorm ways you can improve the experience of buying from your business. Successful customer service standards – those that make your customers *buy* – are:

- **Consistent**. The standards are up kept by every person in your organization. Expectations are clear and followed through. Customers know what to expect, and choose your business because of those expectations.

- **Convenient**. It is nearly effortless for the customer to spend money at your place of business. Convenience can take many forms – location, product selection, value-added services like delivery – and it is also consistent.

- **Customer-Driven**. The service the customer receives is exactly how they would like to be treated when buying your product or service. It is reflective of your target market, and appropriate to their lifestyle. Customers would probably not appreciate white linen tablecloths at a fast food restaurant, but they would appreciate a 2-minutes or less guarantee.

Newsletters: Keep In Touch With Your Customers

A regular newsletter is an easy, time-effective, and inexpensive marketing strategy to implement. Unfortunately, many small businesses think these are too time consuming and too expensive to adopt as part of their marketing strategy.

The most popular type of newsletter distribution is email. This will cost your business as little at $10 per month for an email marketing service subscription, and can be customized to your unique branding.

Here is an easy five-step process to starting a company newsletter:

1. Pick Your Audience. New customers? Market segment? Existing customers?

2. Choose What You're Going To Say. Company news? Feature product? New offer?

3. Determine How You're Going To Say It. Articles? Bullet points? Pictures?

4. Decide How It's Going To Get To Your Audience. Email? Mail? In-store?

5. Track Your Results. How many people opened it, read it and took action?

Value Added Service: Give Them Happy Surprises

Adding value to your business is an effective way of getting your customers back. Every person I know would choose a mattress store that offered free delivery over one that did not. It's that simple.

There are many ways to add value to your business, including:

- **Feature Your Expertise.** Use your knowledge to provide additional value to your customers. Offer a free consumer guide or report with every purchase.

- **Add Convenience Services.** Offer a service that makes their purchase easier, or more convenient. The best example of this is free shipping or delivery.

- **Package Complementary Services**. Packaging like items together creates an increase in perceived value. This is great for start-up kits.

- **Offer New Products Or Services**. Feature top of the line or exclusive products, available only at your business. Offer a new service or profile a new staff member with niche expertise.

Value added services generate repeat customers in one of two ways:

1. Impress Them On Their First Visit. Impress your customer with great service, a product that meets their needs, and then wow them with something extra that they weren't expecting. Get them to associate the experience of dealing with your business with happy surprises, and create a perception of higher value.

2. Entice Them To Come Back. The introduction of a new value-added service can be enough to convince a customer to buy from you again. Their initial purchase established a trust and knowledge of your business and its processes. They will want to "be included" in anything new you have to offer – especially if there is exclusivity. It is easier to attract clients that have purchased from you than potential clients who have not.

Customer Loyalty Programs: Give them incentives

Another simple way to keep in touch with existing customers and keep them coming back to you is to create a customer loyalty program.

These programs do not have to be complicated or costly, and are relatively easy to maintain once they have been implemented. These programs help you gain more information on your customers and their purchasing habits.

Here are some examples of simple loyalty programs that you can implement:

- **Free product or service.** Give them every 10th (or 6th) product or service free. Produce stamp cards with your logo and contact information on it.
- **Reward dollars.** Give them a certain percentage of their purchase back in money that can only be spent in-store. Produce "funny money" with your logo and brand.

- **Rewards points.** Give them a certain number of points for every dollar they spend. These points can be spent in-store, or on special items you bring in for points only.

- **Membership amenities.** Give members access to VIP amenities that are not available to other customers. Produce member cards or give out member numbers.

Remember that in order for this strategy to work, you and your team have to understand and promote it. The program in itself becomes a product that you sell.

8

Profiting from Internet Marketing

Is your business online? If not, it should be.

The internet is today's primary consumer research tool. If your business does not have an online presence, it is harder for customers to find and choose your business over the competition. With over 73% of North Americans online, it is no wonder that individuals and businesses in all industries are looking to the internet to enhance their marketing strategies.

Luckily, it has never been easier to establish and maintain a comprehensive online presence. Internet marketing, also referred to as online marketing, online advertising or e-marketing, is the fastest growing medium for marketing. But it is not just company websites that users are viewing. Blogs, consumer reviews, chat rooms and a variety of social media are growing rapidly in popularity.

The internet is a very powerful tool for businesses if used strategically and effectively. It can be a cost saving alternative to traditional marketing approaches, and may be the most effective way to communicate with your target consumer.

A major advantage of the internet is that you are always open. Users can access your business 24 hours a day, 7 days a week, and depending on your business and the purpose of the website, visitors can also purchase goods at any time.

Internet Marketing for Everyone

The internet is a great way to create product and brand awareness, develop relationships with consumers and share and exchange information. You can't afford not be taking advantage of online marketing opportunities because your competition is likely already there.

Internet marketing can take on many different forms. By creating maintaining a website for your business, you are reaching out to a new consumer base. You can have full control over the messaging that users are receiving and has a global reach.

Internet marketing can be very cost effective. If you have a strong email database of your customers, an e-newsletter may be cheaper and more effective than post mail. You can deliver time sensitive materials immediately and can update your subscribers instantaneously.

See the table on the next page showing the top 10 websites by traffic count in 2013/

You will notice that half of these websites are search engines or commercial sites. An increasing number of consumers are first

84

Table 9 Top 11 Global Websites

from Alexia Internet Rankings May 2013

Site	Domain	Type
Google	google.com	Search
Facebook	facebook.com	Social Networking
YouTube	youtube.com	Video-Sharing
Yahoo!	yahoo.com	Search
Baidu	baidu.com	Search
Wikipedia	wikipedia.org	Reference
Tencent QQ	qq.com	Search, Commerce, Social Networking
LinkedIn	Linkedin.com	Social Neworking
Twitter	twitter.com	Microblogging / Instant Messaging / Social Media
Amazon.com	amazon.com	Commerce

researching products, services and companies online, whether it be to compare products, complete a sale, or look for a future employer. Most people in the 18-35 age group obtain all of their information online—including news, weather, product research, etc. The remaining sites are interactive sites where users can upload information for social networking, or information sharing.

Internet Marketing Strategies

Internet marketing – like all other elements of your marketing campaign – needs to have clear goals and objectives. Creating brand and product awareness will not happen overnight so it is important to budget accordingly, ensuring there is money set aside for maintenance of the website and analytics.

Be flexible with ideas and options—do your research first, try out different options, then test and measure the results. Metrics and evaluations can be updated almost immediately and should be monitored regularly. By keeping an eye out for what online marketing strategies are working and which are not, it will be easier to create a balanced portfolio of marketing techniques. You might find that in certain geographical areas, certain marketing strategies are more effective than others.

This list is by no means the full extent of options available for marketing online, but it is a good place to start when deciding which options are best suited to your company.

Create a Website

The primary use for the internet is information-seeking, so you should provide consumers with information about your company first hand. You have more control over your branding and messaging and can also collect visitor information to determine what types of internet users are accessing your website.

Search Engine Optimization (SEO)

Since search engines comprise 50% of the most visited sites globally, you can go through your website to make it more search engine friendly with the aim to increase your organic search listing. An organic search listing refers to listings in search engine results that appear in order or relevance to the entered search terms.

You may wish to repeat key words multiple times throughout your website and write the copy on your site not only with the end reader in mind, but also search engines.

Remember when you design your website that any text that appears in Flash format is not recognized by search engines. If your entire website is built on a Flash platform, then you will have a poor organic search listing.

Pay-Per-Click Advertising

If you find that visitors access your website after searching for it first on a search engine, then it may be beneficial to advertise on these websites and bid on keywords associated with your company.

These advertisements will appear at the top of the page or along the left side of the search results on a search engine. You can have control over the specific geographic area you wish to target, set a monthly budget and have the option on only being charged when a user clicks on your link.

Online Directories

Listing your business in an online directory can be an inexpensive and effective online marketing strategy. However, you need to be able to distinguish your company from the plethora of competitors that may exist. Likely, you will need to complement this strategy with other brand awareness campaigns.

Online Ads (i.e. Banner Ads On Other Websites)

These advertisements can have positive or negative effects based on the reputation and consumer perception of the website on which you are advertising. These ads should be treated similar to print ads you may place in local newspapers or other publications.

Online Videos

With the growing popularity of sites such as You Tube, it is evident that people love researching online and being able to find video clips of the information they are seeking. Depending on your small business, you may want to upload informational videos or tutorials about your products or services.

Blogging

Blogging can be a fun and interactive way to communicate with users. A blog is traditionally a website maintained by an individual user that has regular entries, similar to a diary. These entries can be commentary, descriptions of events, pictures, videos, and more. Companies can use blogging as a way to keep users updated on current information and allow them to post comments on your blog. If blogging is something you wish to invest in, make sure that it is regularly updated and monitored.

Top 10 Mistakes to Avoid

1 – Failure to measure ROI

Which metrics are you using? Are your visitors actually motivated to purchase or sign up? If the benefits of your online campaign are not greater than the costs incurred, then you may wish to re-evaluate your strategy.

2 – Poor Web Design

This can leave a poor impression of your company on the visitor. A poor design could result in frustration on the visitors' part if they are not able to easily find what they went on your site to search for and also does not build trust. If consumers do not trust your company or your website, you will not be able to complete the sale and develop a longer relationship with that customer. You also need to include privacy protection and security when building trust.

This also includes ensuring all information on the website is current and having customer service available if users are experiencing difficulty or cannot find the information they are seeking. This could be as simple as providing a 'Contact Us' email or phone number for support.

3 – Becoming Locked Into An Advertising Strategy Early

Remember your marketing mix when creating a marketing strategy and avoid putting all of your eggs in one basket. Online marketing is a very valuable tool, but depending on your business and your target markets, other marketing campaigns may be the best option for you. Especially if this is your first time making a significant investment into your online sector, you want to remain flexible and able to adapt your strategy based off feedback received by researching and analyzing different options.

4 – Acting Without Researching

Similar to becoming locked into an advertising strategy early, this mistake implies not dutifully testing and researching different online marketing options. For example, if your target consumer is aged 65+ and you are spending all of your marketing efforts into creating a blogging website (where the average ages of bloggers are 18-35), then you are likely not going to have a successful campaign.

5 – Assuming More Visitors Means More Sales

You have to go back to your original goals and the purpose of your company. More visitors may not mean more sales if your website is used primarily for information and consumers purchase their products elsewhere. This is also vice versa. You could have an increase in sales without an increase in unique visitors if your current consumer base is very loyal and willing to spend lots of money.

Often people will collect information online about products they wish to purchase because it is easier to compare options, but they purchase in person. Even though shopping online is becoming quite popular, people still prefer to see and feel the physical product before purchasing.

6 – Failing To Follow Up With Customers That Purchase

Return sales can account for up to 60% of total revenue. It's no wonder that organizations are always trying to maintain loyal customers and may have customer relationship management systems in place. It is easier to get a happy customer to purchase again than it is to get a new customer to purchase once.

7 – Not Incorporating Online Marketing Into The Business Plan

By ensuring that your online marketing plan is fully integrated and accurately represents your organization's overall goals and objectives, the business plan will be more comprehensive and encompassing.

91

8 – Trying To Discover Your Own Best Practices

It is very beneficial to use trial and error to determine the best online strategy from your company, but do not be afraid to do your research and learn from what others have already figured out. There will be many cases where someone was in a very similar position as you and they may have some suggestions and secrets that they wish to share. Researching in advance can save a great deal of time and money.

9 – Spending Too Much Too Fast

Although it may be cheaper than traditional marketing approaches, internet marketing does have its costs. You have to consider the software and hardware designs, maintenance, distribution, supply chain management, and the time that will be required. You don't want to spend your entire marketing budget all at once.

10 – Getting Distracted By Metrics That Are Not Relevant

As discussed in the following section, there are endless reports and measurables that you can analyze to determine the effectiveness of your campaign. You will need to establish which measurables are actually relevant to your marketing.

Testing and Measuring Online

As with any element of your marketing campaign, you will need to track your results and measure them against your investment. Otherwise, how will you know if your online marketing is successful?

These results - or metrics – need to be recorded and analyzed as to how they impact your overall return on investment.

Some examples of metrics are:

- New account setups
- Conversion rates
- Page stickiness
- Contact Us form completion

Due to the popularity in online marketing and the importance of having a strong web presence, companies have demanded more sophisticated tracking tools and metrics for their online activities. It can be very difficult to not only know what to measure, but also HOW to measure.

Thankfully, it is easier than ever to get the information you need with the many types of software and services available, including Google Analytics, which are free and relatively accurate.

9 Metrics to Track

The following are the key measurables to watch for when testing and measuring your internet marketing efforts:

1 – Conversions

How many leads has your online presence generated, and of those leads, how many were turned into sales? Ultimately, your campaign needs to have a positive impact on your business.

Regardless of the specific purpose of the campaign – from lead generation and service sign-up, to blog entries – you need to know how many customers are taking the desired action in response to your efforts. Your tracking tool will be able to provide you with this information

2 – Spend

If you are not making a profit – or at least breaking even – from your internet marketing efforts, then you need to change your strategy. Redistribute your financial resources and reconsider your motives and objectives for your online campaign.

An easy way to do this analysis is to divide your total spend by conversions. This could also be broken down by product. You could also use tracking tool and view reports on the 'per visit value of every click,' from every type of source. Your sources can include organic/search engine referrals, direct visit (i.e. person typed your web address into their address bar), or email/newsletter.

3 – Attention

You need to keep a close eye on how much attention you are getting on your website. One of the best ways to analyze this would be to compare unique visitors to page views per visit to time on site. How many people are visiting, how many pages they are viewing, what pages they are viewing, and how much time they are spending on the site.

A unique visitor is any one person who visits the website in a given amount of time. For example, if Evelyn visits her online banking website daily for an entire month, over that one month period, she is considered to be one unique visitor (not 30 visitors).

You may also want to incorporate referring source as well – the places online that refer customers to your website. You'll be able to determine what referring sources offer the 'best' visitors.

4 – Top Referrals

Know who is doing the best job of referring clients to your website – and note how they are doing this. Is it the prominence of the link? Positioning? Reputation of the referring company?

Understanding where the majority of your visitors are coming from will allow you focus on those types of sources when you increase your referral sites. They also allow you to gain a better understanding of your online market – and target audience.

5 – Bounce Rate

The bounce rate is the number of people who visit the homepage of your website, but do not visit other pages. If you have a high bounce rate, you either have all the necessary information on your homepage, or you are not giving your customers a reason to click further. In Google Analytics, view the 'content' or 'pages' report and view the column stating bounce rate.

6 – Errors

It is very important to track the errors that visitors receive while trying to access or view your website. For example, if someone links to your website, but makes a spelling error in typing the link, your users will see an error page in their browser, and will not ultimately make it to your website.

You can also receive reports on errors that customer's make when trying to type in your website address in their browser. You may wish to buy the domains with common spelling mistakes, and link those addresses to you true homepage. This will increase overall traffic and potential conversions.

8 - Onsite Search Terms

If you have a 'search website' function on your website, it is useful to monitor which terms users are most frequently searching. This can provide valuable insight into the user friendliness of your site and your website's navigation system. This information will be included in the traffic reporting tool.

9 - Bailout Rates

If you provide users with the option to purchase something on your website (i.e. shopping cart), then you can track where along the purchasing process people decided not to go through with the sale.

This could be at the first step of receiving the order summary and total, or further when stating shipping options. By obtaining this information, a company can reorganize or revamp their website to make the sales process more fluid and possibly encourage more purchases.

Here are the three main questions you should be asking yourself when evaluating your website presence:

1. Who visits my website?
2. Where do visitors come from?
3. Which pages are viewed?

9

Profits Through
Building a T.E.A.M.
(Together Everyone Achieves More)

The people you employ contribute – directly or indirectly – on a daily basis to the strength and vitality of your business. You can't run your business alone, so you rely on their skills and support. In simpler words, your employees help you to make money. But your employees are not just the people who arrive at your office every day and exchange effort for a paycheck.

Your employees are part of a potentially powerful group of people that you must leverage to put your business on the fast track to success. Your staff is more than the people who work for you. They are actually members of your team – the group of people who are collectively working to achieve the same objective, or reach the same vision.

The success of your vision is directly linked to how you engage your team, involve your team and use your team to make growth in sales happen. We know at the heart of successful relationship building is communication, the ability to listen and reflect on ideas and issues.

People make the vision come alive in their daily actions and decisions. Enter any highly successful and profitable business and you will find the people live the vision and values on a daily basis in their actions and decisions. Communication and relationship building go hand in hand and directly impact your success. While this is self evident, this is often overlooked as one of the core elements of business success.

The Alchemist Professors offer a series of tools and techniques to discover your competencies in these areas. It is important to keep in mind the value of an effective team offers additional outcomes and individual efforts.

We all know that more people working on the same task will ensure the task is completed faster. In business, when you have more people working together on the same task or projects doing different but coordinated tasks, you save time, increase brainpower, and ultimately, **make more money**.

Business Culture

Business Culture has become a common buzzword when it comes to building a successful business, and rightly so. It is important to remember that the culture of your business reflects the dominant mindset of its leaders. This mindset is expressed in the culture of your business in style of decision, conflict management, relationship building and ultimately the behaviours of individuals and teams.

In simple terms, your business culture is the environment in which you run your business, and the environment in which your team members work. It is rooted in the vision, mission and beliefs of the organization, and dictates the "kind of office" and "kind of people" that work in that office.

Business culture is something that typically develops organically. The business owner and senior employees create a positive or negative environment based solely on who they are as people and how they behave as leaders. You simply can't avoid creating some type of corporate culture when you run a business.

You can, however, avoid creating a potentially unproductive culture. Whether you are just starting out, or seeking to improve your workplace, you have control over the type of business environment in which you run your business.

In our practice, we consistently find that having leaders who are "authentic" -- being faithful to themselves and their values -- is key to long term business success. As a consistently effective and productive leader you enter relationships and manage performance using authenticity

No judgment is made on the veracity of the values you bring to business. Rather, do you consistently behave in ways consistent with those values? Your values are reflected in your default mindset, the natural and often effortless part of your daily communications and decision-making as a leader

Developing an awareness of your comfort to be authentic and using that in your daily actions, is a core service we offer at Alchemist Professors. We will help you to gain perspective and ability to live your values, to bring about the change you desire in such a manner that your values are honored. Walking the talk of authenticity means just that – living what you say and do. *The heart of authenticity is being present and mindful of others.* Will others see a consistency in your words and action? Consider: the degree of credibility you possess with others on your team?"

With well-articulated values and mission and with authenticity in your actions and decision, you will create a culture that can foster high performing teams to achieve your goals. Like most things in business, this won't happen overnight. However, with a clear idea of where you want to go, and what you want to create, you will be well on your way to getting there.

Vision

Your company's vision statement should be a bold, clear, short sentence that every single one of your employees knows and understands. It is a statement of your intended journey over a set period of time as a business. It is a roadmap to your idea of success; if you don't know what that looks like, how will you know when you achieve it?

If your goal is to create a highly profitable company – what does highly profitable mean? $1 million in annual sales? $3 million in annual profit? You should be specific about the amount and the timeframe, e.g. "We will achieve $5 million in annual sales within 5 years."

Do you seek to become the industry leader in sprocket production? How will this be measured? How many sprockets will you have to produce to reach this goal?

The vision statement is a short summary of the long-term objective of the company. What the company will look like, produce, achieve; it is how you know the company is "successful." Many companies either do not have a vision statement or they keep it a secret from their employees. It is only discussed in board meetings or management meetings.

For a team to collectively work toward a goal, they need to know what the big picture objective is. They need to have buy-in in the company's direction, and be communicated with on a regular basis.

Be proud of your vision. Keep it visible for staff – post it on the wall, include it in internal communications, and connect day to day activities too it as often as possible.

Sample Vision Statements

Here are some real examples of corporate vision statements:

> *"At Microsoft, our mission and values are to help people and businesses through the world realize their potential." – Microsoft*

> *"Give every customer a reason to believe...STAPLES Business Depot—That was easy!" – Staples Canada*
> *"To build the largest and most complete Amateur Radio community site on the Internet." – eHam.net*

Our vision is:

The Alchemist Professors are committed to Growth- our own and our clients.

We do this by honoring the following values:

Empowerment for all involved –us, our staff, our clients and their support networks. Empowerment ensures engagement through engagement we can achieve much more.

Education leads to growth. Knowledge has power. We are committed to continual learning so that we have the knowledge you need and are able to share with you information, learning that meets your just in time requirements.

Sustainability refers to growth and development. We, the Alchemists want to ensure that the change is undertaken such that it becomes the foundation for future change and development. It is sustainable.

Community -The Alchemists is a community of Change agents. The change occurs within the communities of those we work with. We are committed to bettering the communities in which we work. We contribute 10% of our work to community projects.

Creating a Vision Statement

The process of creating a vision statement is something that you can work through alone, or in collaboration with your team. It is highly recommended to review the draft vision statement with your employees to ensure they understand and support the goals and objectives of the company.

Keep the following points in mind when crafting your vision statement:

- **Think Big** – Why did you start or buy this business? What was your dream or purpose in doing so?
- **Think Long-Term** – Vision statements should last five to 10 or even 25 years
- **Be Specific** – Use clearly articulated numbers, dates, ratings systems and other ways of measuring success
- **Be Succinct** – Use clear, short, simple sentences that are easy to repeat and remember

Mission

Your mission statement is a general description of how you are going to achieve your vision. This is a longer and more detailed statement that should include what your business is, who your customers are, and how you are different from (better than!) the competition.

Sample Mission Statements

Corporate Alchemy and the Alchemist Professors mission statement is: *to facilitate the development of our clients in a set of progressive "best practice" competencies for leaders who are consistently effective in teams and organizations.*

"The Mission of McGill University is the advancement of learning through teaching, scholarship and service to society: by offering to outstanding undergraduate and graduate students the best education available; by carrying out scholarly activities judged to be excellent when measured against the highest international standards; and by providing service to society in those ways for which we are well-suited by virtue of our academic strengths." – McGill University, Montreal, Canada

"Starbucks purchases and roasts high-quality whole bean coffees and sells them along with fresh, rich-brewed, Italian style espresso beverages, a variety of pastries and confections, and coffee-related accessories and equipment -- primarily through its company-operated retail stores. In addition to sales through our company-operated retail stores, Starbucks sells whole bean coffees through a specialty sales group and supermarkets. Additionally, Starbucks produces and sells bottled Frappuccino® coffee drink and a line of premium ice creams through its joint venture partnerships and offers a line of innovative premium teas produced by its wholly owned subsidiary, Tazo Tea Company. The Company's objective is to establish Starbucks as the most recognized and respected brand in the world." – Starbucks

106

Creating Your Mission Statement:

Here is a recommended process for completing your mission statement:

> **Step One**: List your company's core strengths and weaknesses; what do you do well? What do you need to work on, or avoid doing?
>
> **Step Two**: Who are your primary customers? Describe the types of customers you serve – both internal and external.
>
> **Step Three**: What do your customers think of your strengths? What strengths are most important to them? Go ahead and ask them if you need to.
>
> **Step Four:** Connect the strength that each customer values with its customer type. Write it in a sentence. Combine any redundancies.
>
> **Step Five:** Organize your sentences in order of importance
>
> **Step Six:** Combine your sentences into a paragraph or two. Elaborate on points as needed. This is your draft mission statement.
>
> **Step Six:** Consult with your staff and customers, and ask for their feedback. Do employees support the statement? Can they act on it? Do customers want to do business with a company with this mission statement? Does it make sense?
>
> **Step Seven:** Incorporate the feedback received, and refine

the statement until you are happy with it. Then publish it – everywhere.

Culture or Values Statements

The Alchemists' Mission and Vision are value-driven. If they were not we would need to develop a cultures or value statement. Your culture or values statement is the next step in the process. It describes how you and your staff will go about taking action (your mission statement) to achieve your objective (your vision statement).

Much like every family has their own belief system and way of doing things – from cooking to cleaning to raising kids – every company has their own set of values when it comes to running a business. It reflects the unique personality of the organization.

Sample Culture Statement

Our Culture

* Values-based leadership. Our Credo outlines the values that provide the foundation of how we act as a corporation and as individual employees so that we continue to put the needs of the people we serve first.

* Diversity. It's our individual differences that make us stronger as a whole. We recognize the strength and value that comes when collaborative relationships are built between people of different ages, race, gender, religion, nationality, sexual orientation, physical ability, thinking style, personal backgrounds and all other attributes that make each person unique.

* Innovation. True innovation can only be fostered within a supportive environment that values calculated risk in order to achieve the maximum

108

reward. At Johnson & Johnson Inc., we encourage and reward innovative thinking, innovative solutions and an innovative approach in all that we do.

* Passion. The deep desire to enrich people's lives – by delivering quality products and remarkable experiences that make their lives easier, healthier and more joyful.

* Collaboration. The unwavering belief that great results depend on the ability to create trusting relationships.

* Courage. The fearless pursuit of the unproven, unknown possibility – the willingness to take great risks for the benefit of the greater good.

- Johnson & Johnson Canada

Creating Your Culture Statement

Involve your team in creating your company's culture or values statement. Generally, this is a point-form document that reflects the beliefs of the company, its employees, and its customers.

It can be helpful to think about the type of people you currently employ, as well as the ones you may wish to employ. What are they like? What are their belief systems? What are their most important values?

Remember that the culture or values statement is usually the longest of the three statements – and that's okay.

Your Team Leaders

The strength of your team lies in the strength of the people who lead it. No group of people is effective without strong leadership, just like no business is effective without a strong owner or management team.

Building a strong team means knowing who your leaders are – both in job description and natural ability. The Alchemist Professors work with organizations and leaders to ensure the following cornerstones of leadership are aligned and in support of their mission.

We focus on five key cornerstones for leadership and change.

1. **Self Awareness:** Fostering the ability to critically self-reflect on the taken-for-granted assumptions informing our views, experience and decisions is the approach we take to assist you in developing greater self-awareness. This will involves a rigorous identification of our assumptions, considering opposite assumptions and evidence to support the opposite assumption. Becoming mindful of the breadth and scope of assumptions is at the core of self awareness.

   Self-awareness is where it all starts- to know thyself is the first step in effective leadership. This is never a completed task. Often the leader feels they no longer need to develop and learn, however research and our experience shows that if you continually engage in knowing yourself and the impact your self has on others the better equipped you are to successfully lead change.

2. **Relationship Building:** Leading change is all about developing the supportive relationships that create sustainable change. The relationships within the group and external to the group you are leading nurtures engagement of others in the vision.

Communication and relationship building go hand in hand. Mutuality and trust are the *core* building blocks of this set of competencies. Identifying the role power plays in all relationships and understanding how this influences stakeholders is the foundation of relationship building. Actively questioning and reflecting back to a person an understanding of their perspective (whether we agree or not with the perspective) fosters communication.

3. **Operational Stretch:** Operational *stretch* competencies include *developing* behavioural and technical *competencies*. Delegation, conflict resolution, decision-making, motivation, project management and influencing behaviours are *core competencies*. No matter the approach or techniques you may choose to follow to develop each of the *competency areas*, *their development* is *part* a life-long learning process and requires constant review and maintenance.

Consider: How often do you update your abilities in these areas? Not having the competencies within the team needed to effectively implement a change can derail the change process.

4. **Leading Strategy Into Action:**

Strategy is by far the most challenging competency. The ability to scan the business environment, question the assumptions used to make sense of the environment demonstrate a level of confidence to define in simple, easily understood language a sense of "magnetic north" is at the core of this competency. If you sampled my team, would they be able to convey back to you a consistent, simple, straightforward and easily understood statement of your strategy?

5. **Authenticity:** It starts and ends with Authenticity. *Authenticity is being present and mindful of others.* Will others see a consistency in your words and action? What degree of credibility do you possess with others on your team?

The change is for you to gain perspective and ability to live your values, to bring about the change you desire in such a manner that your values are honored. You need to walk the talk. Walking the talk means living what you say and do.

Understanding the strength of your natural leaders and the skills of your natural followers will allow you to strategically structure your team for maximum effectiveness and efficiency. It will give you insight into who is best suited for management promotions and project management; which team members have the ability to motivate their peers.

Your leaders need to have a high degree of passion for your product or service, and truly believe in the company's vision. They need to be able to handle a high level of responsibility, and manage a range of people to achieve a common goal. Your leaders are your team builders. They present new ideas, build consensus, and encourage the involvement of others.

Types of Leaders

There are four generally recognized types, or styles, of leaders. Chances are, you've experienced each type at some point in your career:

- **Autocratic**
- **Bureaucratic**
- **Laissez-Faire**
- **Democratic**

Table 10 Leadership Styles

Description	Ideal Use
Autocratic	
Classical or "old-school" approach Manager holds all power and decision-making authority No employee consultation or input Orders are obeyed Rewards/punishment structure	New, untrained employees Detailed orders and instructions are required No other leadership style has been effective Limited time available Department restructuring High production requirements
Bureaucratic	
"By the book" approach All is done to specific procedures & policies All tasks outside policies referred to higher management	Routine tasks performed Standards and procedures need to be communicated regularly Safety or training Cash handling Dangerous equipment

Description	Ideal Use
Laissez Faire	
"Hands-off" approach Employees have almost total freedom Little direction or guidance is provided Employees must make own decisions, set own goals Employees must solve own problems	Highly skilled and experienced employees Employees are highly driven and ambitious Consultants are being managed Employees are trustworthy
Democratic	
"Participatory approach" Employees part of decision making process Employees well informed Leader has final say, but involved others Collaborative approach Encourages employee development with guidance and assistance from leader Leader recognizes and rewards achievement	Collaborative environment Employee development and growth is the focus Changes or problems affect employees and require their input to create a solution Team building and participation is encouraged

Communication

The only way to build and maintain a strong team is through strong, consistent communication. This is often an overlooked or neglected aspect of business management, and is easily forgotten during periods of high stress or heavy workload.

Avoid letting communication go to the backburner. Create a regular meeting schedule – and stick to it. Depending on the size and type of your business, daily, weekly, or monthly team meetings are an important cornerstone of a strong team.

Regularly scheduled team meetings are like Sunday dinners with a busy family. They give you – the owner – a regular forum with your staff to implement company-wide training initiatives, announce results, establish goals and targets, or share new visions or directions. They also give your staff a forum to share feedback and air grievances.

Effective Team Meetings

By now you're probably thinking, "Sure, I hear some company's team meetings are effective, but we tried them and it didn't work," or "I held regular team meetings, but after a while, no one showed up." Successful meeting require people to "show up" in person but also psychological. If a benefit can be drawn from a meeting, people will "show up" and be engaged. If you are an authentic leader, declaring the obvious lack of involvement and seeking support from the team drives commitment. You might say "I am concerned or puzzled by the lack of action" as a starting point/ Creating an opportunity to explore the thoughts and viewpoints from all in your team leads to the potential for more productive meeting outcomes.. This may be a steep learning curve for most so do not hesitate to contact us and get our support in creating the culture that will let you lead a world leading organization.

There is a difference between team meetings held for the sake of having team meetings, and well prepared team meetings with a purpose.

You need to start holding team meetings with a purpose.

Establish a Schedule That Everyone Can Commit To

Scheduling is potentially the biggest challenge when trying to set up a team meeting. Often, all of your staff members are busy going in eight different directions to fulfill their roles and operating on dramatically different schedules.

This is one reason why regular team meetings are important. Ad hoc meetings require ad hoc scheduling, and reduce the likelihood that all your team members will be able to attend.

Ask your team to block off one hour (or two) each week (or month) for the team meeting in a time slot that is convenient for everyone. Establish a clear attendance expectation from everyone. This will exclude that time slot from the scheduling of other meetings and avoid conflict.

If you find that a team meeting is not necessary one week, you can always cancel it.

Know Your Purpose

Each team meeting should have a purpose and clear objectives. Is it to educate? Build consensus? Gather feedback? One of the key roles for a leader to play in the meeting is to question and LISTEN. It is a time for you to learn from your team and for your team to learn from each other.

Once you have established a purpose for a particular meeting, send an agenda to your staff confirming the meeting and outlining your objectives. This is a good time to ask if anyone has a subject they would like to raise at the meeting.

If you find you do not have a clear purpose or objective, ask yourself if a team meeting is the best use of time for that week and consider postponing it to the next regularly scheduled time slot.

Plan Each and Every Minute

The biggest complaint from employees about team meetings is the length. Too often team meetings run out of control, and end up taking three hours instead of one. You will quickly lose team focus and respect for the regular meeting this way. By establishing a clear agenda and staying on topic, you can run an efficient, succinct meeting.

Your detailed agenda should include:

- Meeting purpose or objective
- List of topics and associated speakers
- List of decisions that need to be made/agreed to
- Time allocation for each topic
- Opportunity for additional topics at the end

Circulate your draft agenda in advance of the meeting, and request input and feedback. When all team members have reviewed and contributed to the agenda, you will increase their level of ownership and buy-in into the process.

Establish the Facilitator

Choose one person to chair the meeting and keep it on track. This is generally the business owner or a senior member of the team with some authority over junior staff and a high level of respect.

It is the responsibility of the facilitator – or chairperson – to create an environment of open dialogue and trust, and to keep the meeting on schedule. If you wish to grow future leaders consider having the facilitator's role rotate.

Create a Follow-up Schedule

Assign the task of taking detailed meeting minutes to a team member – or rotate this responsibility on a regular basis. It is important to record what happens in team meetings, just as you would in a client-related business meeting. In the minutes, establish a system for tracking the action items that arise from decisions made in the meeting. This can be set up as a simple chart:

Table 11 Follow-Up Schedule Table

Decision	Action	Responsibility	Deadline

Make sure that these responsibilities are assigned and agreed-upon in the meeting, and clear deadlines are established. Reviewing or following up on this chart can serve as a regular topic during team meetings.

Circulate meeting minutes to all attendees and ask for input or revisions. You may wish to circulate meeting minutes with the agenda for the next team meeting, and gather feedback at the same time.

Motivations & Incentives

A big challenge in team building is coming up with new ways to foster and maintain a high level of motivation. How do you keep teams of people excited and driven to succeed over long periods of time? How do you keep your team motivated to improve their performance, and increase their achievements? Value alignment goes a long way as does empowering people to have voice and impact.

It is important to note that we're not just talking about individuals, but teams of people working together. It is fairly simple to motivate a single person, but an entire team of motivated people will generate significantly higher results. These factors motivate team members if the leader is willing to listen, to create space for open discussion and make tough decisions in keeping with the vision and mission of the company. An authentic leader creates an team culture where authenticity is values.

Before we start talking about monetary and incentive-based rewards, it's important to look at motivational factors that are not incentive-driven. The key here is to give incentives for individual and team accomplishments. Incentives that reward based on collective achievement require people to work together and motivate each other to succeed.

Room to Work – Empowerment

Employees who feel their managers and supervisors believe and trust in their abilities are happier and will always perform at a higher level than those who do not. They are motivated to "prove them right" and feel supported in their efforts.

Micromanagement quickly reduces morale. It is essential that you and your managers clearly express confidence in your team members. You hired them to do a job, perform a role, so you must ensure they have the space to do so.

When you put effective systems in place and establish clear expectations, you create a clear context- values mission competencies and acceptable behaviours or boundary system for employees to work within. They understand the decision-making hierarchy, and the general way 'things are done around here.'

Your team should be encouraged to take initiative and to take risks within this context. You have hired your team based on their skills and intellectual capabilities, and thus should be able to trust in their choices and decision making abilities.

Incentives

Incentives are great motivators. For many the incentive does not need to be monetary but is the ability to have impact and to be recognized. An incentive is a reason to perform or act in a certain way. Contrary to what you may think more money is not as much a motivator as lack of it is a demotivator. Instead of offering a cash incentive, for example, if your team increases sales by 40% by month's end, they will be treated to an expensive dinner with their spouses.

Incentives need to be specific and have deadlines in order to be effective. In the example above, sales need to increase by 40% by the end of the month in order for the team to receive their dinner. If sales only increase by 30%, or if they increase by 40% at the end of the second month, the team does not earn their reward.

Time-specific incentives increase the sense of urgency, and encourage staff to work harder to achieve the objective. If the incentive is not time-bound, there is no reason to work faster or harder, since staff will assume they will reach their milestone "eventually."

Rarity is also a key component of effective incentive-based team building. If the reward is ongoing (i.e., if staff receive an expensive dinner every month sales are over $75,000), then "there's always next time." There is a lesser incentive to push performance to receive the reward. Some team members may care one month, but not the next. Some may not care about a certain reward but may care about another.

Monetary Incentives

Sales personalities respond the most to bonuses increases are a popular way to give your team an incentive to perform. These can include:

- Commissions
- Bonuses for completing a challenging project, or hitting a target
- Rewards for highest producing employee

It's up to you how you choose to structure your monetary incentives, based on your budget and resources. Remember to ensure that the terms of each incentive are clearly outlined, and that both parties (you and your employee) understand the agreement.

Gift Rewards

Physical, tangible gifts are an inexpensive way to reward your team for achievements and improvement. These rewards show that you have given some level of thought to what they might enjoy or appreciate in exchange for a job well done. They're also a great way to surprise employees.

Here are some ideas:

- Spa gift certificates
- Books – *consider motivational or business-related topics*
- CDs or DVDs
- Meals – lunch or breakfast
- Other gift certificates – gas, food, meals, local shops
- Movie or theatre tickets
- Weekend getaway – hotel, meals, etc.
- Flowers
- Gym memberships

10

Buying a Business Successfully

This may seem like an odd topic to include in a small business marketing program. Chances are, if you've purchased this program you already have a business you are focused on growing, right?.

Buying a business is not just about purchasing an already established organization, avoiding start-up costs, and focusing on growth. It's about buying *customers*. Whether you're buying your competition or an organization that offers a complementary product or service, the purpose of buying an existing business is to grow your own base of loyal clients.

That said, buying an existing business is not for everyone, or every business owner. It can be a complex process, with no guarantees of a profitable outcome. You may increase your overhead dramatically in the short term, with no guarantee for a dramatic increase in profit in the long term.

There is also no guarantee that you will secure the clients you are after, or be able to transfer every contract. It may not be the best strategy to grow within your industry, or market conditions. On the other hand, it could be the smartest business decision you've ever made. After all, when the stakes are higher, so are the rewards.

Mergers & Acquisitions

There are two basic ways to use another organization as a vehicle for business growth:

1. **You can *acquire* the organization by purchasing the business outright;** depending on the nature of your agreement, you will purchase their customers, employees, property, etc.

2. **You can *merge* with the organization to create a new business;** depending on the nature of your agreement, you will combine and own half of your customers, employees, property, etc.

Many business owners choose to acquire their target business, and retain control of all business decisions. Alternately, merging with another organization will typically see both business owners in partnership – equally bearing the challenge of joining two companies as one. As you will see throughout this chapter, the choices involved in business transactions will be entirely dependent on your specific business, and your unique goals and objectives for its growth.

In general, here are some advantages and disadvantages to consider when evaluating how a merger or acquisition may help your business growth.

The Acquisition Process

The process of finding and acquiring (or merging with) a new business can be highly time-consuming, but also highly rewarding. The following is a guide to help you find, negotiate with, and acquire an organization that will enhance your existing business.

Finding the Ideal Business

You may have already located an ideal business for purchase. The announcement that the particular business is for sale may have prompted you to consider an acquisition as part of your growth Strategy. Or, you may be considering the idea of a merger or acquisition, and not sure which organization would be an ideal target. Either way, you will need to assess if your target is truly a diamond in the rough, or just a bad egg.

Table 12 Mergers & Acquisitions Pros & Cons

Mergers + Acquisitions: Advantages

- Addition of new employees and skills
- Addition of new knowledge within industry sector
- Acquisition of customers within new market segment
- Increase in market share
- Potential reduction in competition
- Potential reduction in overhead
- Addition of business intelligence
- Gain in tangible assets, as well as intangible assets
- Potential growth in revenue and market presence
- Ability to further develop products or services
- Increase in diversification of business, increasing protection from fluctuation of market cycles

Mergers + Acquisitions: Challenges

- Impact of new management on existing employees
- Impact of old management's exit strategy
- Time management and business performance challenges while agreement is being put together
- Reputation of new business (positive or negative)
- Integration of two staff groups
- Management of compensation and bonus structures
- Integration of two sets of systems and processes
- Impact of new systems and processes on old/new employees
- Relationship building between new staff and existing management
- Impact on existing customer base

A good target to look at is another business that sells complementary or competing products or services, and for one reason or another is not realizing its true potential in the market. For example, you would consider a business under seemingly poor management, or in need of relocation. Often these floundering businesses will need simple fixes, like relocation, a surge of new investment capital, or implementation of new systems. Depending on the seller's motivations, these businesses can also be acquired at a relatively low cost.

You will want to ensure that you undertake a comprehensive due diligence process (to be discussed in the next section) in order to confirm your assumptions, and to uncover any information that the owner has not volunteered.

On the other hand, **a bad target** is a business that sells complementary or competing products or services to yours and is performing well. These businesses have a solid customer base, are making a handsome profit, and under solid management. These businesses will likely expect a high sum in an acquisition, and may not see a benefit in a merger.

Seller's motivations

When evaluating potential businesses for sale, take into account the seller's motivations. This will influence the negotiation process, and will also provide insight into the daily operations of the business. If the business in question is in a complementary market to your own, this can also give you a 'heads up' that upward trends could be shifting.

- **Personal**: owner's health, family problems, divorce, finances, retirement

- **Financial**: bankruptcy, no access to capital, profit levels have peaked, increase in operating costs, increase in professional costs (accounting, legal, etc.)

- **Market**: trends declining, increase in competition, technology out of date
- **Location**: end of lease, high crime area, new non-complementary development, increase in rent

Where do you find businesses on the market?

The answer to this question is a tricky one. Generally, businesses that are good targets won't be listed for sale, which is why the number once source for locating an ideal business is often through word of mouth. But you should look at all possibilities.

1. **Word of Mouth.** If you're in the market to acquire a new business, let your closest or best-connected colleagues and associates know. Word of mouth is the best way to get in on a potential deal early – before others catch on to your ideal target and create a bidding war. Tap into networking events in related industries, as well as the networks of your accountant, lawyer, and other advisors.

Keep your eyes open and be aware of how your competitors are faring in the marketplace.

Key clues that may indicate a business ripe for the picking:

    a. Customer complaints about the competition

    b. Competitor's employees applying at your business for work

    c. Suspiciously low prices

    d. Senior staff leaving the business

2. **Brokers**. Brokers can be a great help to your business search, especially if you have limited time to invest in the acquisition process. Get a quote for their services up front – they will expect a commission from the transaction. Remember, there are lots of brokers out there, so try to get a referral from someone you trust.

3. **Commercial Investment Magazines.** These publications are found mostly in major cities, and list businesses for sale that are attached to property. Retail businesses and apartment buildings are the primary type of organization for sale.

4. **Trade Publications.** These are great resources for businesses that are looking to break into a new industry or marketplace with an acquisition. Their classifieds section will often list businesses for sale.

5. **Online**. The Internet and online classifieds sites like Craigslist and www.Pin.ca are another great source for business listings, especially if you are looking to acquire a business outside of your region. Be wary of information you exchange online, however. You may wish to set up an initial meeting to ensure the lead you a pursuing is legitimate.

6. **Newspapers.** Newspapers can be another source for business listings by category, but also include a high number of scams. Again, be wary when investigating these leads.

This is a **Buyer Beware** time. Make sure you exercise due diligence. Look at everything skeptically. If something smells fishy run away.

Your Acquisition Team

Once you have found your ideal target business, certainly before you make contact with them, it is critical that you assemble a team of advisors to help you navigate through the acquisition process.

Many business owners are wary of engaging expert advice due to the cost involved, which can be substantial. However, it is highly preferable to spend money early on to avoid massive financial surprises after you've signed on the dotted line.

It is a good idea to source your accountant and lawyer – if you don't already have one – from business associates that you trust. These people will need to have an intimate understanding of your business, and keep your best interests at the forefront.

Ensure that you have clear scope of work agreements, and understand the fee structure with each member of the acquisition team. Also, since everyone will have to work collaboratively, it's a good idea to have a face-to-face meeting with the entire team to establish relationships early on.

Table 13 Acquisition Team Responsibilities

Accountant	Lawyer
Valuation Target business selection Financial rational for selection Financial forecasting Financing Review of target business financials Liaison with legal team	Lead due diligence process Draft and review purchase and sale agreement Draft a review business contracts, including employee contracts All relevant legal processes Review of warranties and indemnities

Due Diligence & Valuation: How much is it really worth?

After you have identified an ideal target business, approached the owner or broker, and secured their interest in purchase negotiations, the real work begins.

With the assistance of your acquisition teams, you and seller will need to determine the value of the business in question, and arrive at a price based on that value. The process that establishes how much the business is worth is called *valuation*.

The other critical process you will need to begin is the *due diligence process*. This will help you determine whether this is a good acquisition for your business objectives.

Valuation

The process for placing a dollar value on a business is a complex one. There are many different formulas that can be used – depending on the business in question, whether it is service-based or product-based, new or old, etc. – but each of the formulas are impacted by the hard and soft factors described below.

Hard factors are the tangible assets the company owns. This can include property, buildings, inventory, technology and equipment. These items are fairly simple to attach a fixed price to, and are typically included on the company's financial statements.

Soft factors are the intangible assets that can be attributed to the company. This can include goodwill, location, brand name recognition, and intellectual property – including employees. These factors are complex variables in the valuation formula, and can increase the value of the business dramatically.

Generally speaking, intangible assets are worth what they bring into the company and are valued based on their potential earnings.

Due Diligence

Simply put, the onus is on you and your acquisition team to ensure that the information you receive from the seller is honest and accurate. Failing to do so could cost you hundreds of thousands of dollars after the sale – so don't learn the hard way.

While you can assume the seller is doing their best to provide honest and accurate information, the fact remains that they are looking out for their best interests, and not yours. Therefore, it is your responsibility to gather the information you need to property assess the deal before you enter into negotiations.

Your accountant and lawyer will be able to guide you through the due diligence process, and indicate which financial statements, legal documentation, and bylaws need to be reviewed.

You will need to do your own due diligence to validate intangible assets like goodwill, reputation, and brand awareness. Do not hesitate to talk to their customers, vendors, and anyone else who deals with the company on a regular basis.

Again, your acquisition team should be able to ensure you cover your bases when completing your due diligence. Here is a list of questions you'll want to include:

- How accurate are the financials? Are there any factors that could have falsely inflated or deflated the numbers?

- How realistic are the costs of the products or services? Is there enough or too much allocated to the profit margin?

- What is the true value of the business's inventory? Which items in stock can be realistically sold? Which will need to be discounted and moved quickly?

- Are the lead generation numbers accurate? How many customers are actually walking in the doors?

- Is there any information that the seller isn't volunteering that could impact the vitality of the business?

- Step back and review everything. Are there any discrepancies that don't make sense? Don't rely on the seller's firm handshake or look in the seller's eye. This is your money and your future. Look at the worst-case scenario as well as the best.

Negotiations

Once you have completed a thorough due diligence and valuation process, the next step is negotiations. You and the seller may have agreed on a loose price for the business, but you still have many other issues to discuss and ultimately cement in a contract form.

A key element to be aware of during the negotiation process is intangible assets. These assets can significantly increase the price of the business during the valuation period, so what guarantees will be implemented to ensure those assets continue to earn at the same level?

Here are some other thoughts to keep in mind when negotiating with the seller:

Always Be Prepared To Walk Away. Establish a maximum dollar figure you are prepared to spend on the business, and stick to it.

Don't Get Emotionally Involved. Remember that this is a business transaction that may or may not work out. Once your heart or emotional self is attached the deal, it's easy to spend too much, or give up too much.

Establish A Continuous Flow Of Communication. Make a strong effort to keep communication flowing throughout the negotiation process. Avoid using your lawyer to pass on negative or confrontational messages. Stay calm, and stick to fact-based negotiation.

Focus On Intangible Assets. As mentioned above, these assets can quickly inflate the value of a business, and give the seller certain tax benefits. Make sure that every intangible asset is accurately measured and can be reasonably guaranteed to perform after the seller is out of the picture.

Purchase Agreement

The purchase agreement – or buy-sell agreement – puts the agreed-to price and purchase terms in formal, legal contract format. It is important to remember that this is often the only contract, so you will want to ensure it encompasses every possible scenario to protect your interest. Your legal team will be responsible for drafting and reviewing this.

This document will look different depending on the type of business, and the unique considerations that pertain to the terms of the sale. For example, if you are purchasing assets or shares in company, the structure of the legal documentation will be dramatically different.

Here are some elements that you should be aware of:

Asset-Only Purchase vs. Corporate Purchase – If you buy an unincorporated business or if you buy only the assets of a corporation debts and other legal liabilities generally do not transfer over. If you purchase the shares of a corporation you purchase the whole thing including any taxes owed, back pay and withholding taxes for employees along with any debt. There are tax and other consequences that you need to understand before you complete the purchase. There are pros and cons to each situation.

Warranties. These are essential elements of the purchase agreement. Warranty clauses confirm facts about the business as represented by the seller. These can include assets, liabilities, employees, legal claims, creditors, debtors, and year-end accounts. For example, a warranty clause could state that all outstanding bills have been paid.

Indemnities. Indemnity clauses ensure the seller will pay for unforeseen liabilities related to the business prior to the sale. These could include potential lawsuits, and other costs related to the management of the company before you acquired it.

Overlap period. You may wish to include a clause that will allow you to work in the business for a period of time before the final closing. This would give you an opportunity to identify any major issues that would affect the sale, before the deal is sealed. A bailout clause would accompany the overlap period.

Other contracts. Be aware of other contracts the company you are purchasing is engaged in – including employment agreements, leases, and licenses. You will need to be aware of and review these contracts before you sign the final agreement.

Non-compete clause. This will prevent the seller from establishing a competitive business in the same local area or market. If you a buying a consultancy – where the majority of the value of the business is goodwill – you will want to ensure the non-compete clause is present. It is important to write non-compete clauses correctly or they may become unenforceable in court.

Employees + Customers

After you've signed on the dotted line, you can turn your focus to growing the new business! The existing employees and customers are two groups of important stakeholders that you will need to communicate, build a relationship, and establish rapport with.

Customer retention

If you have just purchased a new business for expansion, chances are your new customer base is of high value to you. In most cases, these customers will have an existing relationship with the previous business owner, and may not be willing or excited to deal with new management. I suggest you spend time getting to know your new clients, and working to establish new relationships and confidence in the new management team. Remember that you may lose some clients, but with effective communication and patience, you will retain the best ones.

Staff retention

The purchase or sale of a business can create much unnecessary strife for staff members. Without fluid communication, the rumor mill takes over and supercharges feelings of uncertainty, change and threats to employment. These things can be damaging to your ability to be an effective manager, so take the time to communicate openly with staff at every opportunity, and involve them in key decision making to earn their buy-in to the process.

Combining policies and systems

Depending on the integration level of the two businesses (old and new) you will want to establish some consistency in the policies and systems of each business. At the very least, you will want to ensure the financial accounting systems are synchronized and systemized to facilitate efficient reporting. At the staff and customer level, ensure that all changes (add, remove or change systems) are clearly discussed, and opportunities for feedback are given. Remember that these changes won't happen overnight, so be patient!

Afterword

From Syd, Larry and Shawn,

So, Where Do You Go From Here?

Take Action! If you're already an accomplished business owner and earning in excess of $250,000 or $500,000 per year, use this book to learn how to make it grow to a Million Dollar Business. If you are not as accomplished as you would like to be then the best thing to do is to concentrate on strategies to LEARN and the EARN will follow!

If you are serious about taking the next step then go to work on yourself, study other business successes, understand marketing strategies and become a sponge for new (proven) material. The amazing thing about the game of business is that when you put proven processes to work and continue to follow them, an abundance of success will follow. The biggest mistake is to start a process and then fall back into your old habits after a short time.

Above all, get the knowledge you need before you step onto the field. Think about it…if you were going play hockey one-on-one against Bobby Orr or Wayne Gretzky, wouldn't it make sense to learn the game and practice before you stepped on the ice to play them? It is amazing to us how many new small businesspeople start the game of business against seasoned professionals (the competition), without first developing the necessary knowledge to be successful. Then they fail and blame the market, the economy, their location, etc.

If you have a business and have not yet managed to start to create wealth and systems that allow you to take time off, build retirement accounts or pay for your children's college, then learn and master the steps outlined in my book. We, the Alchemist Professors, are very much advocates of education and mentorships. Get the right information, find someone who knows how to walk you through the steps and watch your quality of life take new shape.

For a Free Test Drive of all our best tips, tricks and marketing resources, visit www.AlchemistBusinessAcademy.com

About the Authors

Sydney Scott

Syd has been a University Dean and has started up two MBA programs at Canadian Universities. She currently resides in North Vancouver, BC with her son and his family and a very large dog.

Larry Earnhart

Larry has been a serial entrepreneur after working in the U.S. chemical production industry. He also teaches Business courses at University Canada West. He lives in Victoria, BC with his tween-age son.

Shawn Ireland

Shawn has an ongoing international consulting practice and teaches MBA students at University Canada West. He is the author of *IFRAME: A Managers Guide to Critically Balanced Thinking.* He resides in Vancouver, BC.

Alexandra Pett

Alex has lived in Eastern Canada, Alberta and the West Coast on Pender I Island and now resides in Victoria, BC. She is a writer, painter and professor of English at University Canada West and is the author of *Transforming Selves under the Gaze of Others: Evolving Traditions in Life-Writing.*

The Alchemist Professors
www.TheAlchemistProfessors.com

15230495R00092

Made in the USA
San Bernardino, CA
24 September 2014